Joyce Stranger was born in London but has always lived with animals and taken a keen interest in wild life. She started writing at a very early age and is now the author of best-selling novels, mainly based on her own experiences with animals. She also writes many children's books (one of which, *Jason*, has been filmed by Walt Disney) and some non-fiction, including *Two's Company* and this book, *Three's a Pack*, which describe her life with her Golden Retriever, Janus, and her two German Shepherd bitches, Puma and Chita. Joyce Stranger also writes for several magazines, such as *Dog World*, *Dog Training Weekly*, *Off Lead* and *Gamekeeper and Countryside*.

Her life revolves totally around animals: she rides every week, and she runs a dog training club which has a variety of dogs of all breeds. Of her own dogs, Puma (who died recently) won a Championship Certificate in Breed; Janus has won a number of places in Obedience, and Chita is being trained for Working Trials and will hopefully also compete in Obedience.

Joyce Stranger has five grandchildren and four step-grandchildren, and lives in a 300-year-old cottage in Anglesey.

Also by Joyce Stranger

THREE'S A PACK

JOYCE STRANGER

CORGI BOOKS
A DIVISION OF TRANSWORLD PUBLISHERS LTD

THREE'S A PACK

A CORGI BOOK 0 552 11951 2

Originally published in Great Britain by
Michael Joseph Ltd.

PRINTING HISTORY
Michael Joseph edition published 1980
Corgi edition published 1982

This book is set in 10/11 Monophoto Plantin

Corgi Books are published by
Transworld Publishers Ltd.,
Century House, 61-63 Uxbridge Road,
Ealing, London, W5 5SA

Made and printed in United States of America by
Offset Paperbacks, Dallas, Pennsylvania.

This book can only be dedicated to CHITA,
the fiendish puppy that exhausted me,
gave me the challenge of my life,
and now repays me, beyond measure,
for all that I suffered on her behalf.

I owe thanks to Edith Nicholls for reading this manuscript professionally for me before I submitted it to my publisher.

I also owe thanks to John Cree, who is always patient and helpful when I phone; and to the many serving police-dog and railway-dog handlers who have offered me help and advice, as they are my only link with Working Trials.

Chapter One

This is the story of my own dog.

I have no ulterior motive in writing it. I write about my animals. I wrote about Kym, my Siamese cat, some years ago. I wrote about my golden retriever, Janus, and my German Shepherd, Puma, in *Two's Company*.

I intended to write about my present pup long before I bought her. I wanted her for Working Trials, a new field to me; and I wanted to write about our progress towards that goal.

The agreement that I signed when I bought her, as I always make sure that everything is down on paper, reads, towards the end:

'The pup will be a pet; to be trained hopefully for Working Trials and Obedience, and also shown in Breed, always providing I am able to travel with her and not deterred by ill health.

She has the lines I want and her mother has the temperament I need, but I am well aware that even then she may not be a show dog; or even a working dog. From my point of view that will not matter a great deal, as basically I want her for a house pet to take over when my two older dogs are no longer here.'

I signed that when she was eight weeks old.

In fact, as always with a new puppy, she did not turn out quite as I hoped. She proved to have far too great a predomination of working lines; something I had never considered, as I hadn't met it before. Something few breeders consider, as they don't always realise it is possible to have too much working strain, or too little; and either way provides the owner with difficulties in certain circumstances.

One criticism levelled at me, often by dog breeders and competition people as well, who don't know me personally, is that as I write fiction, I live permanently in the realms of fantasy.

Every writer knows that fiction is *not* fantasy. In my case, much of my fiction is hard basic fact, based on intensive research, which I always do personally. I don't use research agencies. I am a trained research worker myself. I have a Science degree (B.Sc.) which doesn't predispose one to fantasy.

I worked as a medical research worker for four years at ICI. I had a boss who, when I showed him my results, said, "Have you checked? Well, check again."

"Did you look it up in *The Lancet*?" he'd ask.

"Yes."

"What about the American medical journals? And the German? And did you cross-check with the veterinary journals to see if there was any reference there? Go back and look properly."

During the next twenty years, I spent many hours of my life watching wild animals in their own habitats, investigating animal behaviour: foxes, running and hunting in the fields. Badgers, from a hide; deer, from a hide. I tamed a small hawk: I spent every hour I could afford away from my desk and my family responsibilities among farmers, among gamekeepers, among men who shoot and among police-dog handlers; at dog shows and at sheepdog trials; at small gymkhanas, riding, pony trekking, mucking out stables, going round the farm helping bottle-feed a litter of pigs or an orphan lamb; standing with the hot velvet knobs of a little tame deer held in my hands because my hands were cool; his velvet was throbbing and very hot: I stood against a tree watching an osprey struggle with a trout that was too big for him. He killed it in the end by hammering its head against a rock.

I spent hours in kennels watching puppies of all breeds, as many of my friends breed dogs. My aunt bred Airedales. My son worked for years on a local farm, amongst Jersey cattle; out before early milking, home late at night to dunk his filthy clothes in a bucket in the garage to steep, and later the water benefited my roses. He was always full of farming stories. We both have a passion for Jersey cattle, though I will go miles to avoid a Jersey bull; they aren't usually funny.

I worked out the other day how many hours I had spent at dog clubs in the last nine years, and startled myself by the total. I had a husband who travelled the world. I wanted to go to the theatre, he was in Moscow with a trade delegation, so I went alone. Or I wanted to go to a family wedding. He was in Toronto, or Montreal, or New York; or Munich, Frankfurt, Paris, Geneva, Basle . . . When he came home he was busy, he was tired, and we didn't go anywhere. So in the end I trained my dog to a high standard, as no one comments if you go alone to a dog club, or a dog show, and I enjoy working with animals.

I went to dog clubs, when I lived in Cheshire, on Monday nights, Thursday nights and Friday nights, when I helped teach; and on Sunday mornings, spending four hours there most days. The family were grown up and mostly away from home. It proved fascinating and rewarding, and I learned a good deal about all kinds of dogs.

In these nine years, I have spent over 4,000 hours at dog clubs, among dogs of all breeds, and among all kinds of owners. I have spent over 1,000 hours at dog shows, both Breed and Obedience shows. I've spent about 300 hours at least on various courses, run by top people in the dog world, learning from them; and something like 200 hours learning about all kinds of dog training from various people, including police dog-handlers.

It may sound a fantastic number of hours, but if people only watch TV for two hours an evening, five nights a week, in nine years they will have spent 4,680 hours watching television. It adds up remarkably.

In the last five years I have also spent many evenings helping people train their own dogs.

I am not writing this as a form of bragging, but in the hope that anyone who feels I don't know what I am talking about, or am inventing or fantasising, will realise that my feet are firmly planted on the ground. *I* clear up the dog muck and bath the dog that has rolled in pig dung or a dead sheep. I clear up when the dogs are sick and I nurse them when they are ill. I don't have kennel help of any kind.

I don't profess to know everything about dogs. Nobody ever can.

My dogs live with me, in the house, and travel with me. I don't have a kennel to confine the dog that is irritating as a companion. It must either learn to be livable with, or it goes. I have never yet had a dog that had to go. You can retrain most dogs.

When I visit our vets, I know them well enough to see the dog that has just been run over and lost almost all its leg, and see its progress week by week. I make friends with it so that it greets me when I go there. I may hear of an odd calving, or a new foal, or about the lamb disease that is plaguing the farmers. Or maybe I am told where there is a rare breed of animal, or an unusual litter of pups.

I hear about the odd behaviour of a hundred pet dogs from their owners; some are very clever. I watch owners with dogs that won't behave at all come week after week, and who, one evening, walk in with immense pride with a dog that is now behaving. I learn of family sorrows, some minor, some major, and from time to time get involved.

It is far from being a fantasy world.

I am involved in it, up to the neck. When I write fiction it is never fantasy. That is something only a few can do well; most of us are too firmly rooted on this earth to fly to the stars. The animals in my books are real animals. I don't invent them.

I see them, am fascinated by them, and put them into a book. The background is sometimes real; Puma's breeder's kennels provided all the background for the Paddy Joe books; her dogs were the dogs in *Never Count Apples*.

The lane where Puma's Show handler lived was the lane in *Never Tell a Secret*; his cottage, which he took on as a derelict tumbledown building inhabited by tramps, was the cottage in *The January Queen*.

I first saw it on a summer day when I went to discuss Puma's next show with him. It was a horrible semi-ruin. I sat on the dustbin beside a pile of planks and ate sandwiches. A year later I sat inside a very nice home indeed, to discuss another show, having seen the house develop from something no one would look at twice, to something very comfortable.

The horses in *Breed of Giants* were the Lymm Shires. I stood beside their owner often, watching them; and was told to stand my ground. When the latest colt galloped over and braked hard in front of me, I was sure he would never stop and I wanted to run. His enormous plate-like hooves looked as if they would put an end to both of us. All he wanted was to have his ears rubbed. Their owner was one of England's top breeders and judges. I've only to mention his name to a man who breeds Shires and I'm instantly welcome.

I stood recently in a field watching a half-Arab stallion greet his owner, rather alarmingly, by rearing in the air and putting one hoof on each shoulder. He is a very jealous animal, so that when she came to talk to me, he tried to pull her away, using his mouth on her arm to get her attention. Few other people can handle him and I wouldn't dream of going into his field. He wouldn't tolerate it. He will form part of a book in due course, but I need to watch him more before I put him on paper. Last month, I bought him.

The deer in *Rusty* was the little deer whose antlers I held. Rhua was growing his first antlers when I stayed there; he still insisted on having a bottle every night, in spite of his age, and the lamb that had been reared with him for company did too. Every day his owners said the pair were too old for a bottle, and tonight they were going to learn they had to give it up. They created such a din that in the end the animals got their own way.

The badger in *The Honeywell Badger* was Billy, who played with the dogs and musked my shoe, and was 'worn' by the children round their necks like a scarf. He dug holes in the house and he dug holes in the garden and caused immense problems by escaping.

The foxcub in another book was Susie, who played with a feather as a kitten plays with a straw, and at six months old was gentle, pretty and extremely naughty, biting the dogs if they wouldn't make room on the hearthrug. Her owner had killed a number of foxes the day he found her; and despite the fact that his main occupation was ridding the land of vermin for the local farmers, he had taken the ten-day-old cub home and his bitch had reared her with her pups. People are often inconsistent in their reactions, and surprise one.

So what has this to do with my new puppy?

It has a great deal to do with her, because without such a background I would never have kept her; I would not have known how to cope with her without such a background, which gave me knowledge of some hundreds of dogs. I would never have recognised her for what she was; not a very wicked, half wild pup, but a pup bred to work, and bred so hard on those lines that her babyhood was total frustration. It couldn't be anything else. She was also the most dominant bitch I have ever met.

A baby collie can herd chicks and herd the family without problems, even when untaught. It does no harm. But what do you do with a baby police dog that is programmed by its inheritance to attack? She had to learn, and learn fast; but it's not easy to teach, as without experience, without training, that dog will never learn and may well grow up very dangerous, not because it is dangerous in itself but because it is living the wrong kind of life. Anything a pup does becomes a habit later on; whether it is a good habit or a bad habit depends on its training. Left alone, it teaches itself bad habits and perpetuates instincts. Taught, it can become a very sensible adult.

I had to re-think all I did to give her the right kind of life, which meant changing the way I lived. I had to re-think all I knew about dogs to make sure I knew how to cope with her. She was outside my experience.

I know now, through talking to others, that she is outside theirs too. Very few people have met a dog that is so strongly bred to work, it is like a high-powered engine that can never be turned off. Or so forthright that even as a pup it will challenge a very dominant adult dog.

My pup needed to be taught, she needed to be doing, but she wasn't mature enough to cope with training to the extent that would have helped her. Only when she reached maturity and understood that working was what she was born for, was enormous fun, did she begin to be easy to manage or to handle.

Now, if she feels energetic she comes and butts me. "Come on, let's do some training."

I pick up her slip chain and lead and before I can put the chain on her she has jumped into it and is sitting looking at me.

"Come on, what are we doing today? Can I jump? Can I track? Can I search? Shall I 'stay'?"

Out on our field she is waiting all the time for something interesting to do. She carries home letters, carries the newspapers, digs flat the molehills, will fetch a quoit back to me endlessly, ready to go on long after I am tired.

She will search and search and search again, looking for her toys; find things the other dogs leave on the field and bring them to me. In the evenings she leans against me 'talking' with her eyes, long soul-searching conversations that go on for ever. If she wants something badly she comes and looks at me, knowing I will follow her, maybe to her empty waterbowl, maybe to the back door as she needs to go out, maybe to Janus, who has decided he needs cheese and is sitting, willing the refrigerator door to open.

My dogs make sure I live in a world of hard fact. No fiction for them. They are aware of time; time to go out; time to be trained; time to get ready for the dog club; time for food. Time in the morning to get us up and go out on the field, and come in again for their morning snacks.

Time for walks. Time for the beach or the country. Time for a journey to visit friends, or a show. They have their own needs and their own ways of making those needs known. The older ones prepared me for this little one; without that long background she would definitely not be here and I would have missed out on a very interesting animal.

This book is mostly about Chita. It is factual and unexaggerated, and to prove that I include letters from a number of people who know us. Some only briefly, but whoever meets Chita gains a lasting impression as she has tremendous character.

I wrote to the German Shepherd Improvement Society about Chita; and was told that many of her type of breeding were as difficult as she, as youngsters; and I was asked, if I found out how to control her, if I would let them know.

This book is for the German Shepherd Improvement Society. I think it has value to them above all, as it is a fair account of one dog from very hard working-breeding, as opposed to breeding for the pet market. It is not a criticism of the dogs in her ancestry; nor is it intended as criticism of her breeder, who tried to get a dog with obedience capabilities; no one could tell how the mating would turn out.

No one can predict or guarantee anything in breeding; heredity isn't like that. A dog long forgotten may lie, far back, in the pedigree of both the sire and the dam, and the two sets of factors may come together to produce a throwback, a total freak.

Buying a pup is a chancy business; no one can say with absolute certainty that it will turn out well, even with all the care in the world. Careless breeding rarely produces good pups. Training can overcome major defects; lack of training will turn minor problems into major defects.

I hope that all who read this book will read it as intended; the story of one pup; the totally true story of one pup. It is not intended as anything else, but hopefully, it may help breeders to know how these pups turn out; and it may help owners to persist, to train, and, in the end, to turn their own apparently unruly pups into dogs that are beyond any dog they have ever known. It doesn't happen by chance. It's very hard work – but it's worth it.

Chapter Two

There are breeders who never train a dog, and know nothing about living in a home with only one or two dogs, which is very different from having kennels in which you put the dog that is a nuisance in the house, and forget it other than feeding it and maybe using it as a stud dog, or breeding pups from it if a bitch, or selling it to someone else, not mentioning that *you* found it unfit to live with.

The problem goes on, just as it does when dogs are rescued, or new homes are found because the dog bit or behaved badly. Why should someone else inherit the dog *you* have ruined, or the dog that should never have been bred in the first place? Get it put down and stop the problem – don't wish it on some other innocent with too soft a heart (and head).

I am writing about *my* dog. Not any other member of her litter; not any other dog from the same breeding. She is unique, which is probably just as well. No way would *I* breed from her, as all the experts whose books I have read say that no matter how you breed, you can't breed out nervousness, shyness or vice; they are all dominant. Such characteristics prevail in the pups, and to breed on makes matters worse, and worse, and worse still. Chita has been spayed.

Two years after buying her, I decided I wouldn't change her. She is immensely rewarding when she does right; only occasionally is she near to reducing me to canicide, but then she co-operates and I experience a relationship with her that I have never known with a dog before; a load of trouble and a load of fun. People who hated her now like her immensely.

But let me make one thing plain.

I think it highly unlikely that, had she been sold to anyone else, she would be alive today. She gave me a tremendous challenge – and I like challenges. Life without them is life without achievement. I decided that if I gave up with her I would give up a great deal of valuable experience. Also I knew enough about dogs to know that if I could manage to get her under control, I might have something quite exceptional. It hasn't all been happy experience. I have despaired and felt defeated; been angry and been exhausted. I have learned far more than the vast majority of dog owners will ever know.

I hope that those breeding the Alsatian cum German Shepherd will think deeply before mating. What is there? Will the pups be easy for pet owners?

In Switzerland before the last war, there were five types of German Shepherd bred; there may still be; the companion dog, the guard dog, the army dog, the police dog, the guide dog. These were *not* interbred, as what would rate as plus ten for aggression in a police dog is minus ten in a pet dog, and vice versa.

Working dogs need far more occupying, far more deliberate training exercise, and no free running among strange dogs, or they turn out wild. Few pet owners have time or inclination or know-how for this. Even after Chita, perhaps particularly after Chita, I do not feel that I will ever again buy a German Shepherd with working police dogs in its ancestry. If I had been older, I doubt if I could have coped with her at all.

Litters may be bred for wrong reasons; to get a champion, hopefully. But champions are hard to come by or there would be many more of them about. So what happens to the also rans? They are often sold to pet owners, whether suitable or not. What are they? Mated for shape of head and set of tail, mated for a well-laid shoulder and a well-sprung hock; never mind what is in the dog's head. It might be nervous as a wild kitten or savage as a tiger; mad as a March Hare or wild as a vixen. It could be impossible to live with. Half those who use it never know. They see it once, at stud, when it has its mind on other things and is bound to show its best side to the bitch, or she won't tolerate it. It may not be the dog at fault. The bitch has ancestors too.

There are the dogs in the pedigrees the dogs in the history.

I made up a joke pedigree recently to illustrate a lecture on breeding. The dog was named Crazy Mixed-Up Pup, fathered by Devil of Hell, who in turn was fathered by Champion Swinehound of Hell. His mother was Vicious Bitch of Ignoramus. Many people breeding now know nothing about their breed's history; about the villains and the saints; the whole breeding is so mixed up it makes little sense, and what comes out is as unpredictable.

Few now know what lies in the past, but those dogs can come out uppermost; breeding is like that. I've seen the oddest little bitch, related to my own Puma, who lies there well back. I would never have mated her parents together; I would have looked for something quite different. But then maybe I knew things that the breeder didn't, as she was from a pet bitch, not a breeding kennels. These are hidden and well-kept secrets, but before you buy a dog (of any breed) ask questions; lots and lots of questions. Don't ask the breeders. Ask the local vets and their nurses. They know.

Ask at the dog clubs, where the pups come to be trained. They know.

Ask who bought a pup and what happened to it; not today, not yesterday, but a year ago; two years ago. Find out the kennel reputation, not from just a few people, ask around. I never say, 'Don't buy from X.' I just never mention X and suggest going to W, Y and Z. Also remember that people change, and those who bred good animals years ago may have lost their dedication.

Ask to look at all the dogs you can from that breeder. Avoid most dealers – many sell pups from anyone and they know nothing at all about the stock they came from. Until people learn to ask for *good* pups, and they ask questions, the market will be flooded with pups that may cause problems all their lives.

Dogs are always happy on their own territory. You want to see them in strange surroundings, when the nervousness may show: the uneasiness, the wariness, the odd behaviour.

All dogs at home are different dogs. They know the rules and they know the ground and they know how to behave, as circumstances are always the same. What shows up is how they behave when out: distracted, aggressive, nervous, edgy, wary; or balanced and sensible, interested and curious; dogs that are a pleasure to be with.

If you want a dog of any breed, walk in the local parks; ask the owners about it. Everyone is happy to have a dog admired; an owner who has had a raw deal will talk.

Talk to my mother and hear her enthuse about her dog; and about the dog breeder, as her West Highland White is now seven years old. She goes just once a year to her vet for a booster. Her breeder sends a Christmas card every year, and keeps up an interest, wanting to know all about the dog.

Another breeder may well say, "Hell, I haven't time. I don't want to know. The buyers are a nuisance."

That's when the buyer comes to the dog club with a sad tale, needing help that wasn't given, and that's when the dog clubs start their lists of people to buy from.

I tried to get a very easy-tempered pup; everyone tried. No one sets out to produce a devil by sinister intent; it's sheer bad luck. But there are others, like Chita used to be, about. Maybe I can help them and make others think hard about those pedigrees before they buy, because when I took my pup to someone who knew, she identified the joker in her pack without even knowing the pedigree.

"It's not you, it's your dog," she said. "X is in her pedigree, isn't he?"

He is.

She never tells lies about dogs; if it's the owner who is to blame, she says so. Without her, I might well have given up.

This book, as much as anything, is a thank-you to her.

Without her, it might have had a very different ending. And no matter what I do with Chita, whether we win in competition or lose, whether we qualify in trials or not, and I very much hope we might, some of the credit will be Edith's; for the time she put in, for the thought she has put in, and for the experience she has passed on.

I gave up all thought of competition at first. My only aim was to keep her safe and alive. Her impetuousness ran her into one devastating situation after another. I had to work on her. If I hadn't, all the teaching in the world would have been useless. No one else can train *your* dog – and the training must be done *daily* to ensure control.

We are nowhere near the end.

Chita, as I write, is just over two years old; and is coming under control. She is still wildly excitable and apt to forget. She can be touchy, and can be edgy, and can still drive me up the wall and down the other side.

She is a hell of a character.

She is often a hell of a nuisance.

One day she may well be a hell of a great dog.

I don't know. The next book, if we both survive the years that are to come, will tell you that.

Three's A Pack is only the first instalment.

I wonder what the next instalment will be called.

A dog in a million?

Well, she is just that; but whether for good or ill, I don't yet know.

I hope we have de-bugged her; she is safe with everyone and she is very sweet with me.

When she goes, which I now hope and believe will be at the end of a normal span of life, the gap she will leave behind will be out of all proportion.

She has taught me as much about people as she has about dogs. She has furthered my education in ways I never expected; she has changed me completely. In the past, I couldn't have been nearly so firm with a dog; my older two would have been better trained if I had. She has given me a great deal more confidence. If I can cope with Chita for two years, I can cope with almost anything.

Now, when she needs discipline, I don't hesitate. Hesitation with this one would have meant death for her, as it has for so many that were put down because the owners couldn't train them or wouldn't train them.

Is it better to be sweet and gentle and produce a devil

that defies you and ends up dead? Or to be firm, and have a dog that is a pleasure to own? Firmness is *not* cruelty.

Soon after buying Chita, I started to run a training class; oddly, because people kept insisting I was already running a class, which I wasn't. I hadn't even thought of starting a class, as I hadn't the time and I didn't want the responsibility. But, as my phone began to ring non stop, with people asking where the class was, or wanting advice, I decided it would be simpler to hold a class. It confined the training problems to one night a week, instead of their going on throughout the week on my phone.

Training classes bring in all kinds of people with all kinds of dogs, and one very soon finds that one person's interpretation of hard treatment varies according to his own dog. There is no way I could ever be as firm with Puma as I am with Chita. Puma needs far gentler treatment than many smaller dogs, as she cannot bear a harsh voice, or a stern reprimand.

All I need to say to her is "Oh, Puma!", in a very softly reproachful tone, and she is apologetic for the rest of the day.

Janus has always needed a firmer voice. Call to him sweetly and lovingly, when you want him to come, and he looks up and his eyes grin.

"She doesn't mean it." And he goes right on with whatever he is doing, which these days is digging up the ground, looking hopefully for moles, which he never finds; or trying to open the gate and go off on his own affairs. I have to use a no-nonsense voice on him.

With Chita, as with many of her breeding, it is necessary to use a really firm voice. I have had to develop a Chita voice. There was no way whatever that anyone with a soft voice could have got through to her in her early days, when she was deaf to everything, intent on whatever she wanted to do, which was frequently suicidal.

Handled correctly, there is never any trouble. But often, in club, there is a charming, gentle old lady, with a charming, gentle old dog, that has never caused a problem in its life. She is horrified when a young German

20

Shepherd has to be taught manners, and some of them need a great deal of teaching.

John Holmes, who is never cruel to any dog, comments in his book *The Obedient Dog* that he feels very sorry for women with young powerful German Shepherds, as they never have the strength in their arms to deal with the dogs as they should be dealt with.

It does need strength, and plenty of strength. One of our pupils came with his mistress, who had no effect on him whatever, no matter how hard she tried. I suggested one night that his master took the dog; five minutes on the floor reduced him to a panting, sweating, exhausted state, and he has handled the dog ever since. Even then, that dog still needs much more force when being taught, as he exerts all his strength and pits his will against his master.

The methods needed for training a large powerful dog are very different to those needed for training a tiny gentle dog. There are breeds like the Sheltie, that need relatively little training if bred right, as they will walk automatically at heel and don't need teaching to remain there; the gundogs walk automatically a little behind their owners; they are selected deliberately and bred to walk like that, as there they are out of the way of the gun. It means that very often Labradors and spaniels and retrievers get docked in the Obedience ring for lagging. They aren't lagging, in fact; they are doing what they were bred to do. Even so, many pet gundogs pull, because their owners do not know how to check them and they soon learn bad habits.

The German Shepherd racing out and barking at the intruder is not a vicious dog; he is not even necessarily a bold dog. Generations of breeders have selected him for guarding and, because he is a big powerful dog, he must be taught not to over guard, and that teaching can be very hard work.

Pups of this breed start to guard very young; sometimes as young as sixteen weeks. They must be taught from the start that while a certain amount of barking is permissible, it must not go on senselessly. They must not race at innocent visitors and frighten them half to death. They must greet people sensibly; they must behave in a civilised manner.

Teaching them is never easy; some learn fast and some learn slowly, as every dog is different. Every pup in a litter is different. Each of them inherit something different from their parents. Brothers and sisters in a family are never alike, and neither are dogs.

I knew, before I had owned Chita for two weeks, that this pup was like no pup I had ever seen before; and that many of her problems would be caused because others would fail to understand her. She obeys very few people, knowing full well she can play most of them up. Her playing-up is annoying but harmless. She has taught me a great deal that I will never regret learning.

She has re-taught me, above all, that you can never lay down the law with dogs. You can never say "all need teaching this way", or "all need teaching that way", because they don't.

She has taught me to question everything people have said to me, because very often what they said applied to their own dogs and to dogs they had known. They had never known Chita.

Few people have had a dog like Chita. I know very well when I talk to people, even people well experienced with dogs, that they haven't the slightest conception of what it is like to own a dog like this one. The hints they give me are useless. They have never been challenged by a dog so dominant that she fights for her own way, even at eight weeks old.

Janus and Puma, our two older dogs, both had minor problems at first but now both are superb. Great fun to live with and each immensely endearing. Janus is almost nine now; an elderly gentleman with a great deal of character, and a habit of summing-up people very well. He knows which of my visitors he can make fools of.

Puma is the one I can take out and about as she is totally non-aggressive. Village dogs can run up to her and rave at her, and she walks on, ignoring them. Baffled, they stand and look at her and then turn away. Both the others would accept the challenge and might fight. People who are afraid of Alsatians invariably fall in love with Puma. Chita, among people, is even more endearing.

Puma reassures the puppies with her maternal presence: gentle, affectionate, licking the small noses turned up trustingly to her, no matter what breed.

Janus won't tolerate misbehaviour in young fry. He tells them off; a roar to discipline them, but he never bites. People who ought to know better interpret this as bad temper. It isn't. It's the old man keeping the youngster in order; disciplining his pack. Boss of the pack, to be obeyed. It can be very useful.

"Tell that pup off," I say, and Janus roars at her and grins at me, knowing he has put the little one in her place.

Janus took me into the world of Obedience, because he pulled so vigorously that I had to learn how to train him properly. Once I had begun, I discovered that he loved work as long as it was never too much work, and I loved teaching him. We started a long partnership that has now ended as far as competition is concerned, as he is too old for the ring and I can't ask him to perform for me any more. He prefers to remember. He is slower, and a little rheumaticky, and is developing an old man's ways, grunting in annoyance if no one will take any notice of him, pushing against me firmly if he feels it is his turn for attention. He still has his daily stint of training. He demands it.

Puma took me into the world of Breed; of shows for beauty, rather than for intelligence. That was an accident too, as she was bought to replace Janus who was under a death sentence; he had some odd complaint which meant he was never well. I had to be talked into showing her, but when she began to win prizes, I became intrigued.

She ceased to win after gaining a Championship Certificate, as there are now two distinct types of her breed. She is the noble English Alsatian, as near to the standard as any can get.

Dogs shown recently are more like Chita – showing the influence of German imports. They are smaller, darker, and very much leaner in shape. The rift is now so large that a new society has been formed; and a demand has been made to the Kennel Club to acknowledge the fact that the two types are so different they can be considered different breeds. Puma is too old now – a veteran, but maybe if I can show her with her own type she can still win. At the moment it is pointless to try.

Meanwhile, after I bought Puma, we discovered what was wrong with Janus. His pancreas didn't produce the enzyme needed to digest meat; this could be replaced by a powder I put on his food. He has never managed to produce the enzyme, but the powder works well and he is as fit as any dog of his age can be. So, there I was with two dogs.

When we moved, I knew their time in the show ring was limited; and I wanted a new youngster mainly to train, perhaps also to show.

Chita took me into a field I had never expected to enter, that of re-training villains. She wasn't all villain. If she had been, the choice would have been simple. She always adored people, and above all adored Kenneth, my husband, though he was very far from returning her feelings as he detested her at the start. I had been given her, which made refusal difficult. I had promised him I wouldn't buy a pup till the following May. We were going to have the winter free, with older dogs that fitted well into our way of life and needed relatively little attention.

As far as he was concerned, I had broken my promise; and it was hard to explain that it is never easy to refuse a gift. The gift proved to be a very odd animal; and for both our sakes I had to learn how to cope with her. I insisted on paying. Too much can go wrong and I would never feel I was the complete owner of a dog that had been a present. Partnerships rarely work – my dog must be totally mine. It was a good job with this one that she was totally mine.

I wanted to try my hand at Working Trials. I had bought Janus for that but his bad hip defeated me. He could never jump. This one jumped like a kangaroo from the moment I got her. I put up mini jumps, no more than a foot high, on the field, as there at least she could get rid of some of that terrifying energy that prevented her, ever, from settling down and relaxing. She had to be on the move endlessly, and it was very exhausting for everybody but her.

This time round I would try my hand at what has always been to me the best type of competition, as it makes the dog think. I used to watch the hounds hunt on the fox trails, hunting out the scent; and watch the police dogs tracking, practising for the day they would become operational for the first time; hunting out the scent.

Scent on the ground, scent in the air, scent on the wind. Scent. What does the dog smell? I spent long nights thinking about foxes and the way they hunt on a rabbit trail; watching badgers come out of their sets, cast around and go off, noses down. Watching Janus hunt the hedgerow, nose busy, throwing up a pheasant or a partridge and standing waiting, not knowing that he was waiting for the gun I didn't have, to shoot the bird, so that he could bring it back to me.

Instinct strong in him all the time.

Puma doesn't ground-scent; she air-scents. Catch the scent of a squirrel in a tree, hundreds of yards away, and up goes her nose, sniffing the air. Janus, meanwhile, has the scent on the ground and is zig-zagging, to stand under the tree, his nose lifted too now; he never does air scent.

I would sit and watch them home in on the same scent in totally different ways.

Put something on the ground for them to search in long grass and Janus makes a pattern, covering every inch of the ground, though I never trained him to do that. Puma circles, apparently not scenting at all, and then up goes her head and she pounces and brings me her trophy.

Not much of a trophy; an old hankie, or a glove.

I spend hours with them, watching them. They are so different in every way when using their noses. Puma will lift hers if I am away from her and search the wind, Janus will hunt till he strikes my track and follow that. Both reach me together.

My puppy would be taught on police-dog lines. Search and track and jump. I had wanted to do that for more than ten years; had been out with people who did train their own dogs that way. I had watched John Cree, who wrote

Training the Alsatian and who had trained Champion Quest of Ardfern, his own dog, the first Scottish Working Trials champion. I had watched the police dogs, every year since 1969, at their own trials; had been out with dog-handler friends when they trained their dogs; had sat in at 'inquests' on tracks that went wrong. I had done a bit of tracking with Janus who was born to track; with Puma who wasn't and had to be taught.

It would be fun to have a dog from working lines; strong working lines, to train for Working Trials. Jack Cree gave me Dan Hare's fifty-year-old tracking harness. It had been worn by a champion, and Quest had worn it. It was given me for luck – I was going to need luck.

The pup came; I was talked into owning her but the task wasn't difficult as I wanted a new pup very badly.

I thought I had what I wanted; I thought I knew a great deal about training pups; I did all the right things, very carefully, very gently, the way the books said.

I didn't know I had a pup that would have sorted out a big tough man; I had thought Janus dominant; Janus thought he was dominant. Puma was sure of her place in the home. Janus was pack leader, after me; I was his boss and he never forgets it when he is being trained, though he might just try it on if he thinks he can get away with it and change our roles. Luckily, I recognise it, and he quickly changes his mind.

Puma never challenges either of us.

Our pack was already formed.

I, as packleader, Janus as second and Puma the third.

Then we brought a stranger into the pack.

She was determined to be boss: my boss, Kenneth's boss, Janus's boss and Puma's boss.

This was a real pack.

She came into it at eight weeks old, and right from the start began to show me that I knew nothing whatever about dogs, and certainly not about dominant dogs.

She was going to be Boss, come hell or high water.

Only she had problems as I wasn't letting her and nor was Kenneth or Janus.

Her uncle is a police dog. I knew that, but didn't think too hard about it. A working dog. Her great-grandfather fathered very hard dominant dogs, but I didn't know that. Even the best trained of working dogs can develop wrongly. One of the best sheep dogs in Wales died recently. He killed a sheep and his owner shot him.

If that can happen with a trained dog, anything goes with one that no one has trained.

They don't make good pets. Not for them the fireside, and fussing. They will find their own occupation, which may be destroying your home, or barking endlessly as they rush round the garden chasing birds in the sky. They may become obsessional about playing with a stick and go on and on and on, a keen working mind gone wrong.

A deprived dog.

A working police dog is trained daily, six days a week for three months and then he is operational. On duty, he is out and about; he may track endlessly, he will be trained on and re-trained; he will be occupied all the time. Off duty, he will be resting, tired out mentally and physically.

Sell such a pup to a pet owner and he has nothing to do, so he guards like a maniac. He guards his owner when out on the lead – and the car, and the house; and the garden and the drive. He may get free and guard the road outside and chase cars and bicycles off; and people too.

He has ancestors that were trained to attack and he attacks without knowing why; anyone and everyone.

He *must* be trained.

Training is controlling: control the instinct; let him guard when you say so and at no other time; control his passion for barking and control his need to do something, anything that leads him to destroy your property because he is so bored. He needs much more than walking; that doesn't tire his brain, though it may tire his body if you can do it for long enough.

He needs to be taught: to be taught to walk beside you, at heel, to come when called, to drop on command, to stop in mid-chase, or before he has gone flying after 'prey'; to ignore cats and running children. And, if he is a strong minded very dominant dog, he needs to be trained for far longer than the books say; as otherwise, with an active body and an active mind, he will go delinquent.

Training is a routine, worked out to cope with this. You need to go about it the right way, all the time; to learn to train properly; to treat your strong-minded dog as if he were an embryo police dog. Give him mock searches and mock tracks; make his life interesting so that when you rest in the evening his brain is tired and he sleeps too.

All dogs need some time devoted to them, and a working dog far more than most. So make sure your pet dog comes from breeding that has no working ancestry of any kind, as it is downright cruel to deprive such a dog of the training that is needed.

Puma is easy; no working lines dominant in her, so she has never needed more than Breed and pet training.

Chita is something rarely met in a lifetime of dogs.

Training is not easy. Not all trainers teach the same way. Even the professionals may be wrong about your dog. If you read George Summers' book *Living with Dogs* (Arthur Bowler) or Tom Mahir's book *Police Dogs At Work* (Dent), you'd find that in the early 1950's, even the police knew little about the right way to train their dogs.

Tom Mahir in his book pointed out that the early training the dogs had was dangerous, and taught the wrong things.

Police-dog training is very different now. The dog must be under control, by a word, even when running full pelt after a criminal. Under control in all circumstances, at all times.

Since I had a baby police dog, this had to be my aim. I had never before, in all my life, met a dog that pitted her wits against me, constantly, from babyhood. I had that to overcome too. It was going to be very tough indeed and I had very little help, as no one I knew had any experience of a pup like Chita. The majority of people wouldn't have tried. They'd have handed the pup to someone else, or kept it kennelled, or the RSPCA would have put it down.

Chapter Three

I brought the pup home in October.

A grey day with a little rain, my new puppy in the wire cat basket, curled up, glaring at me through remarkably angry, very small eyes, like little boot buttons in a coal black face. I'd suffered that effect too with Kym, my Siamese cat, who was furious after he was sold. My pup had floppy ears that would one day stand erect, small black paws and a tail that refused to wag.

I took her out to the car.

Puma took one look at the basket and retreated to lean against the hatchback. "Take that thing away at once," her expression said.

Janus curled his lip. "What's that? I don't like it."

I had named her Chita. Corgi books said in their introduction to *Kym* that I have two dogs, two cats and a Puma! I had one cat only now, and Janus, and another dog called Puma; so this would be a cheetah, but spelt differently.

"Chita," I said, and put my hand down to her head to stroke her, and re-assure her.

She bit me. Hard, meaning it. She was being stolen, taken to a car stinking of great big strange dogs, she wanted her mum and her litter mates and familiarity, and though I had gone over and played with her, it had never dawned on her (how could it) that one day I would come and tear her away from everything familiar in her eight-week-old world.

She cried; within a few minutes she was in a tantrum, screaming at the top of her voice, and it was a very lusty voice. I stopped the car and picked her up and cuddled her, but she didn't want that; she decided to explore, and had to be put back because the two older dogs didn't like the look of her at all, or the noise she made.

She screamed all the twelve miles to the vet. She

endured her inoculation, sitting moderately quietly in my arms. The vet fussed her; that wasn't too bad. Back in the car, she screamed. I took her on to the lawn where big dogs always went and showed her where she could go; she performed and was praised.

I had a pen for her. I put her in it and she promptly climbed the wire and fell splosh over the top, and rushed into the kitchen, where she yelled. I put her back and put a lid over the top; gave her a bed with a nice soft woolly blanket in it; gave her toys; and newspaper in case she was quicker than I was. Gave her food, which she gobbled fast, older dogs getting a biscuit too so as not to be jealous of her.

They *were* jealous. *That* puppy.

That puppy screamed.

Kenneth came home and hoped she wasn't going to continue to make that din. I went out to get our supper; rattled plates; she screamed. I put her on the lead and took her outside. She did everything a good pup should and in she came and she screamed. And screamed and screamed and screamed. We both had headaches. The two older dogs looked as if they did too. I had never met a puppy that screamed non-stop. I fussed her; she went on screaming. Kenneth stroked her; she bit him.

I took her out of her pen and took her to Puma. "Here's a puppy. Mother it."

"You must be mad," Puma's expression said, as plainly as anything could, as with extreme dignity she walked out of the room, as far as possible from the lunatic little monster continuing to scream at the top of her voice.

It suddenly became clear to me. Chita wanted food, non-stop; and outside, non-stop; and attention, non-stop; and to chew the rug, non-stop; and to chew the electric flex, non-stop, and to create general mayhem, and here was I preventing her. No one was ever going to stop Chita doing what *she* wanted to.

I put her on her lead and gave her a little lesson. Heeling beside me, with a toy in my hand for her to look up at. Her idea of progress was in sharp short dives after the cats.

Casey retreated to the bookcase and swore. He was going to be another problem, as Casey had a mind of his own and if thwarted he would bite her, and bite hard. He would also scratch. Chita (and I suddenly realised how ridiculous it was going to be with a cat called Chia and a pup called Chita) did as Chia always does in her private emergencies; she decided life would be better if she moved for the time being to the wardrobe. It was dark there and the noise was muted.

By now the weather was in tune with Chita and it was blowing a gale. Neither she nor I enjoyed our trips outside, and since the wind was making such a fuss *she* would too; she wouldn't do anything anywhere ever again. She sat on the lawn, about eighteen inches of mutiny and mutinied. Biddable little pup? She glared at me. I pulled on the lead and she rushed in at my leg and bit my ankle.

The books didn't tell me how to deal with my kind of puppy. The books, and I have a good selection, apparently had never heard of my kind of puppy. I made allowances. It was all very new and she probably had tummy-ache; she didn't know me yet and she was afraid of the two big dogs. I cuddled and fussed her and she struggled right out of my arms and went off to see what there was in the way of carpets and cushions to kill.

I put her back in her pen and went to the two big dogs who needed to go out too, who had been very neglected all day, who hadn't even been fed, and who cuddled up against me. "Get rid of it," Janus's eyes said. "Get rid of it," Puma's paw said, beseechingly against my knee.

"Get rid of it," Kenneth shouted, as the screams went on all evening; went on into the night, went on and on and on. Around four in the morning, he announced that either the puppy or I, or perhaps both of us, would land in the river if she didn't shut up.

I had never in my life heard anything so persistent. She was sobbing with pure temper, and nothing I did would stop her. I got up very early and I fed her and took her out and played with her. I cuddled her and fussed her and tried to make her understand she now lived with us. I removed swearing Casey, by now demented with the noise, and tried to get Puma to cuddle her. Puma did lick her, but that was all; she looked haunted, and small wonder.

Somehow Chita had to understand, and understand fast that we would all like her better if she would only stop that noise. It was an eldritch screaming noise; a ripping tearing noise, like a demented heron, only decibels higher. It infringed the laws of sanity and the Noise Abatement Act and it set our teeth on edge. The cats had both departed; the dogs were as far away from her as they could get, and by now it was evident that either I managed to stop the din or I got divorced. I didn't want to give up in twenty-four hours; that would be ridiculous. I didn't want to give up at all. I hadn't had Puma at that age. Maybe all Alsatian puppies behaved like this.

I rang John Cree.

Poor John and poor Irene; their phone turned into a hotline while Chita was small, with me yelling SOS down it time and time again, as no one I knew had ever had a puppy like this one.

Nothing wrong with her physically; and certainly not with her lungs.

"She's a boss dog," John said, "and you have to make her understand right from the first it isn't on. You are boss. Stop her biting and stop her making that noise."

It was easier said than done.

I wrote to Barbara Woodhouse for her book *Training Your Dog My Way*, and there I got my first clue as to what to do. Later I visited Barbara, who agreed Chita was a wild one and gave me half a day of her time, which I appreciated very much.

Pups settle quickly, the books said. The books hadn't met Chita. We had her a week and every night was hideous. I tried warm blankets; I tried no blankets. I tried a ticking clock (mother's heartbeat, they had to be joking). I tried a hot water bottle. I tried scolding and I tried cuddling. I ignored her, and she still went on and on and on. I didn't reward her by going to her, but as she never stopped she probably thought I'd come in answer to a five-hour scream. I went to bed at 1.00am and got up at 5.30am. I was exhausted. She wasn't. Chita yelled by day as well; in her pen; out of her pen. In the car, out of the car.

By the end of the week, it was plain that she had to shut-up or go back.

I made a plan of campaign, having by now phoned everyone I could think of.

I couldn't kennel her – my neighbours would go mad; although they aren't very close I can hear their dogs bark. I prepared to do battle; with a nine-week-old scrap of nothing that seemed in a permanent rage. What was saddest of all, she wasn't a happy puppy, and yet nothing at all had been done to her by us that could account for such bad temper. I hoped I hadn't bought a villain; I had never met any pup like her and I had seen plenty of pups of her breed. They enjoyed life. Chita didn't.

She was in permanent revolt against the world, it wouldn't do as she wanted, she couldn't do as she wanted, and by heaven she was going to be boss over us all and we could lump it.

If I let her free she bit Puma and she bit Janus; and she tried to bite the cats. She didn't seem to have learned that it isn't acceptable to use teeth hard. Maybe it was only puppy play, but it was very painful puppy play and human babies came to the house.

I had looked forward to my pup for two whole years; had planned for her for all her little life in the world. Now I looked at her and wondered what on earth I had got and where it came from. I wondered what the rest of the litter was like. I wished I hadn't succumbed when offered her. I tried to work out what I was doing wrong, but no way could I get a clue as I was doing nothing wrong.

Chita wasn't a puppy at all, she was a hellcat. I had said when things went wrong with Puma that they couldn't go wrong a *third* time, that I would be lucky soon. I looked at my little horror and knew without doubt that you can be unlucky three times in a row, I was stuck with her; but being an awkward sort of person who hates to say no to a challenge, I made up my mind then and there that Chita would be civilised, and end up as good a dog as the other two.

The only snag was *how?*

Dogs aren't human, which is a point many owners forget. They don't think like us and they don't act like us. They respond to triggers and Chita had too many triggers to react to. Food: make a noise. Mistress: make a noise. Janus: make a noise. Puma: make a noise. Chia: make a noise. Casey: make a noise. Birds: make a noise. Door opening: make a noise. Plates clattering: make a noise. Need out: make a noise.

The last was useful except that it was the same noise for everything.

She simply never was quiet, not even for long enough for me to say "Good puppy, quiet puppy," in one of the pauses. There weren't any pauses. She ought to have been exhausted but wasn't. She did stop to eat, but the noise she made while I got her food ready (nothing wrong with her sense of smell either) had to be heard to be believed. The pen careered frantically from side to side of the room with her pushing it, yelling.

One thing; she was far from timid. She was over bold; and too bold for her own good, as she had no sense of caution. Outside, if I didn't watch her, she rushed on the end of her lead to the edge of the four-foot wall and tried to drop over it. She dived into holes and she dashed along narrow planks. We had builders adding a house extension which didn't help. They started the day after I got her, and she delighted in the noises they made; helped the concrete mixer, added her din to the crashing of corrugated iron and the hammering of men and greeted them vociferously at the top of her voice. They roared with laughter. *They* didn't have to live with her. She adored noise. The louder the better.

Sunday. No builders. Kenneth went off to his boat and I started in on Chita. She had to be made to *shut up* for at least long enough for me to say "Quiet, girl. Good girl."

The only thing that ever brought a temporary silence was when someone was making more noise than she was; not by bellowing, as she didn't care if you produced an enormous sergeant major voice. It had no effect on Chita, though Puma, looking haunted, would take flight, hide behind a chair and peep out at intervals, obviously saying "Oh, heavens, please shut her up." Cats decided to live upstairs, even for food, and to come down at high speed to go out and rush in again, ears flat, eyes wild.

Janus finally lost his temper and roared at her. "Shut *up*, you."

She stared in amazement; he had a louder voice than she did and into the blessed silence I said "Good little baby. Good little girl." I stroked her and peace lasted all of half a minute, then she began again. This time she did want to go out, so she got lots of praise. She was very clean indeed, as I concentrated on her needs.

Feeding time approached and silence ended.

I fed her, and she slept for a little. She never slept for long and I wondered if she was having enough food, but she obviously was. Too much, if anything. Had she tummy-ache? Cut it back; get the vet to look at her. Nothing wrong. Just bloody-mindedness.

Right. So into her pen she went and I collected pan lids and things that made all the noise I could think of, put Janus and Puma in the car, as far out of earshot as possible, and set to work.

Fortunately for my peace of mind and other peoples' thoughts on my sanity, we have no neighbours very near, only two chimneys in sight but well away from the house, across a field. We hardly ever hear them; only very occasionally do we hear their dogs. I hope they don't hear us, especially when I am coping with Chita.

Chita screamed. "Want out; want to play. Want to eat shoes, eat hearthrug, bite cats, bite Janus. Want to do things."

I rolled a ball.

"Don't want that. Want to do more interesting things."

35

Crash and yell.

"Bad puppy. Pack it in."

Astounded small black face, head on one side: "She can make a *big* noise. Cor."

Dead silence and into it as fast as I could. "Good girl. Lovely girl. Quiet girl."

"I can make a noise too," says puppy, and starts in. Crash and yell.

Silence and more fast praise. The silence lasted a little longer.

Chita obviously didn't like silence so she started up again.

Crash and yell.

"Isn't that interesting?" She came to the edge of the pen and looked at me with real attention this time. Up to now I had just been there for her convenience, to scream at, or to bite. Not to notice.

I sat down and began to read, all the time saying softly, "Good Girl, *quiet* girl."

Approval didn't seem to register. She began to yell again. I kept it up until I had almost no voice but the pan lids could still crash, and I made it louder and louder. I felt demented; I felt it quite wrong for so minute a pup; I wanted to pick her up and cuddle her; but Chita never wanted to be cuddled, she wanted to be doing, and wriggled till she was on the ground, where she immediately started to make mayhem; she had an inbuilt suicide instinct.

When I walked her round the field she moved in short hard jerks, going from smell to smell.

"Cor, rat . . . weasel . . . mole . . . partridge. Cor, what's that, and over there?"

I began to check her; she didn't care. She was going to do her own thing. Always, no matter what, and do it she would. She was far far worse than Janus had been at first, and much younger. Strong-minded, dominant, I presumably had the litter pack leader. She was a devil, even at that age.

I walked the big dogs; blissfully, silently, sensibly,

leaving puppy in her pen. I played with Janus and I played with Puma. We went in.

Chita screamed with delight. Not alone any more.

She had to learn that no one could live with that noise so out came the pans. Big dogs fled to the sitting-room, and I shut the door. It was obviously going to be a battle of wits and I was so tired; and I had only had her a few days.

That night, she only yelled for half the night, not for all of it. Presumably she was as exhausted as we were. I fell asleep, blissfully around three in the morning, only to be wakened about five by an odd noise that wasn't Chita. It was Puma.

She felt sick.

She was sick; very sick, over and over again. I moved the pup to my study, right away from possible infection, though it was going to be difficult. She had to go outside and I had to handle Puma and puppy. Puma was too ill to go to the vet so he came over. She had an injection but went on being sick all day. By evening, she was a little better. I took her to surgery.

It was Monday and Bristol Show was on Saturday. Puma had one Championship Certificate and I was hoping she might pull off another. But this was a virulent germ, and you can't take any dog to a show that has had an infection within the last six weeks. Furthermore, she could still be infectious; and also she wasn't going to be fit to travel. Nor could I put the puppy in kennels, and she had been booked in, in case she was sickening for the infection. Janus was to stay with Kenneth. But we had to cancel. No Show.

Puma picked up in a couple of days and Janus started in the same way. Luckily, by now I was prepared, and he came over to the vet at once and recovered in twenty-four hours. Puppy seemed unaffected, except she was a little bit loose and needed to go out at two in the morning and four in the morning and six in the morning. So she screamed and told me, which did happen to be useful; except she continued to scream at many other times too.

Her tummy had never been absolutely right from the

37

time I got her, and she also had worms, which didn't help at all. She had been wormed before I got her, but the worming agents don't touch the eggs so if there is a hatch after worming (all puppies are born with worms; they lie dormant inside the bitch till she is in whelp and then shift to the pups) then there is re-infestation.

Worm her. Change her diet. This time on to something quite different, as she had been reared on an all-purpose food. All-purpose foods vary; some are good and some aren't. The fact that food is made for dogs by commercial organisations does not mean it is necessarily good for every dog. Some people are allergic to perfectly ordinary normal foods, like wheat or cow's milk, and dogs vary too. Later we found she was a mild case of pancreatic enzyme deficiency, like Janus.

Most pups have tummy problems when they change to their first home; even if the food is right, stress upsets them. They can't avoid stress; journey in the car or bus or train; different smells; no mum; no litter mates to play with and cuddle against. Just strange people and a strange place, and perhaps not enough sympathy and understanding.

Perhaps. This pup had all the sympathy and understanding in the world. We had done everything to make her welcome. Kenneth did his best accepting the inevitable. But she didn't want to respond. She had one idea only in her small head, an idea that has remained with her for a very long time. She was not a dog that wanted to please anyone; all she wanted to do was please herself. Food won her heart; food was the only way of pleasing Chita.

Both Janus and Puma had been difficult as youngsters in one way or another; Janus because he was stubborn, wilful, extremely independent and dominant; and now I have met people who really know dogs I do know I was right in that estimation; it was never my fault he wasn't under control at first. I needed help and no one knew enough. There are very few people, even today, who can take him *and* control him. He stays my dog, obeying me;

and he plays the rest of the world up doing exactly as he likes. Only *his* playing-up is funny – not wicked.

Puma was only difficult in that she was seventeen months old when she came to me. She was used to her kennel home; never having been in a house, she hated everything in the house; boxes that spoke to her or suddenly blared music or, worse, produced pictures; curtains that swished; refrigerators that growled at her; washing machines that 'shot' her when they changed programmes. Life for Puma for months was traumatic, as nothing in a house was predictable. Lights flashed on and off at whim; fires went on and off apparently by magic; things that were cold sometimes were suddenly hot and burnt her nose.

It was all too much for Puma, but at last she settled too.

So with all that behind me, how could another dog be difficult; and a puppy at that?

I had had dogs before Janus, but he made me re-think all I knew about dogs. Puma, compared to him, was easy. *This* one almost broke my heart.

Nothing seemed to be right for her. She didn't like the older dogs and bit them. They objected, not very surprisingly. She didn't seem to like us; she bit us. She bit people who visited us. She yelled whenever she was stopped from doing something she enjoyed doing. She enjoyed chewing electric flexes; she enjoyed chewing books and letters and shoes. She enjoyed fraying the hearth rug. It is now fringeless, with a moon-shaped piece missing. She enjoyed climbing; out of her pen on to a chair, on to the window-sill, yell at the cats outside; on to the table, to take whatever took her fancy, the more expensive the better; retire and demolish it.

I put a roof over the pen, to stop her climbing out. She fell every time and might have hurt herself badly. She mountaineered up the wire mesh and dropped; flop – on to the hard floor.

She screamed with fury.

"Want out. Want to chase cats. Want to bite big dogs. Want to bite carpet."

By now, the only time there was peace was in the car. She enjoyed movement. I put her in the wire cat cage, in which she was at first lost; I ordered a travelling crate for her, as it soon became plain that if she wanted to get out of the car, she would be out and into the road and under a passing car and very dead indeed. The crate is a wonderful invention.

She had no intention of learning anything whatever . . . except how to please herself. One way she got her own way was to scream for food; it came. It never dawned on her that it came at set times. Screaming at 9.00am did produce food finally at midday, as she already had been fed at 8.00am. I couldn't feed her every half hour which might, just, have shut her up. She was having plenty to eat. The vet thought I might be overfeeding her.

So, into the car, and in her little travelling crate, on the front seat with the lid up, and my hand to stroke her. "Stay down. Good little pup. Stay down." It was more comfortable anyway staying down on her warm rug, so that brought progress. Big progress. In the car to Chita meant *down* very soon, and I was able to keep her by me, reassuring her at intervals, and remembering to say "Stay down, good pup," as I drove.

When I left the car and went into shops or the library, she had the lid fastened firmly, as friends of mine lost a puppy left in the car. He was tied by his lead to the door handle, inside, and he climbed over the back of the passenger seat and broke his neck. That happened at dog club, one night, while their other dogs were being trained, and since then none of those of us who were there at the time have ever left a puppy loose in a car.

Chita, left loose, but right under my eyes, attacked the older dogs; and Janus is *not* patient. She ripped the upholstery and she tried to fall out of the windows. Outside the windows were roads and passing cars, and more ways of death and injury than any pup could dream of. So the lid went down.

Many people thought her big travelling crate was cruel, being unaware that without it this pup would now be dead. Even at two years old, if she wanted out of the car, she was still the very devil to restrain. As far as Chita was concerned, everything had to happen yesterday; she couldn't wait. She wouldn't wait. She would do as she wanted and the hell with everyone else and every other dog. That way, dogs *die*, killed by their own impatience. The older dogs envied Chita her little home. The second I took her out, they wanted to get in, and often I'd find Janus sharing the crate with Chita. "Not got a crate – it's not fair!" It's standard practice in the United States.

It took four weeks for me to realise what I had. One of the hardest and toughest little pups that had ever been bred. In her fifth week with me, tummy now behaving, house-trained, but nowhere near being biddable in any way whatever, she decided her mission in life was to guard. She didn't know what she was guarding but guard she must, and she did it the forthright way; belt down the field at top speed and bite ankles. Anybody's ankles. And since she had remarkably good teeth and destroyed bones that the older dogs had had lying around for weeks, that hurt.

She had to be stopped, and I stopped her by watching her. As she came full pelt (very funny, I suspected she thought), I simply put my foot up so that she met the sole of my shoe. No kick, no movement, she crashed on to an unrewarding hard leather sole, and she did not think that so funny. It took three encounters with my shoe before she decided this was an unrewarding game.

She tried instead to run, leap at hands and bite those. Really bite, not puppy fun. Not puppy nibbles. Bites. I closed her mouth, my hand round it, and said "No," loudly.

You never could use gentle tones on this one when she was intent on mayhem; anyone who tried it was in for a shock, as if you did she knew you were soft as butter and she did her own thing; which caused considerable surprise to the unwary.

"Kiss, kiss," and she nudged her nose against my hand. She learned "Kiss, kiss" most of the time, but hold a biscuit out, or a piece of cheese, and she nearly had my fingers off. We have baby grandchildren and that had to be cured.

I phoned for advice.

"Watch her and, as she tries to bite, thump her under the jaw. Don't mess about; she needs a good hard lesson that she will remember. If she continues to bite, one day she will do major harm (Alsatians have been known to kill children) and that means a short sharp end."

Not coming back from the vet. This became Chita's theme song, and was always in my mind. I got on top of her, or else –

At the time, I still didn't know enough about really tough dogs; I suffered from the delusion fostered by many dog-club trainers, by many people who write dog books and by many competition judges, that all dogs want to please their owners, and if something is wrong, it's the owner, not the dog. So, what was I doing wrong? Why was she so impossible? Why did she bite? My advice seemed to be cruel; it's very hard to hit a pup.

This highly unpleasant and dangerous habit did have to be stopped and after she turned on Janus and bit his ear when he passed her, going busily nowhere except to his bed, and got well and truly roared at by him as his ear was damaged, I decided I *must* stop it. Most pups learned not to bite from their litter mates; bite hard and you got bitten hard back and you didn't do it again. Or mum disciplined them. I wondered if perhaps she had been boss of the litter, every other pup afraid of her, getting her own way all the time. She was a horrible little bully and the older dogs were looking harassed and haunted. Puma spent most of her time behind the settee; Janus spent most of his time curling a lip at the pup, growling under his breath. I dared not leave them together unless I was there. Chita slept alone. The older dogs slept upstairs. I was afraid they might harm this little fiend.

She tried to bite me and I caught her in the act and hit her very hard under the chin as her teeth came up to my hand.

42

Janus reached over and grabbed her ear and bit hard, but he didn't draw blood.

She squealed.

Chita never bit any of us again, except just once, some time later, and that could have been a reflex, unintended. She was in the car with Puma, Janus was at home and I was being entertained to lunch. When I came out, Puma came fast out of the car, crying, crouching low, her tail apparently broken. She wouldn't get back in with Chita. She travelled home on the front seat, in considerable pain, and I went straight to the vet.

"She hasn't broken it, Chita's bitten it." It was a very deep bite. We thought at first that Puma was going to lose more than half her tail, but it did finally heal.

Chita snapped at things that went fast past her head at that stage. Had she snapped without meaning to? I didn't know, but after that she was chained in the car so that she couldn't reach out and bite the older dogs. And I had to cure the snapping; she developed a new fault the second I'd cured an old one.

We had cured her biting. How did I stop her screaming? It still went on; every time she wanted something, and she wanted a lot. She'd want to get out of the car and kill that dog on the pavement; want to chase sheep; want to have dinner, tea, supper, want to have cheese; want Janus's dinner, Puma's dinner. The only time Puma ever did tell her off was at feeding time, as Puma was rapidly becoming the third member of our household pack, not the second, as she should have been with an easier puppy.

Scream. Chita was a headache in every sense of the word.

Kenneth was fed up with her; I had to change my life style, or she would have to go. I went to bed late, and got up very early, and spent most of the days in the car, as at least there she was quiet unless she saw another dog on the pavement. Her yells set Janus off, and I have no doubt whatever that non-dog people were convinced my dogs were fiends. In fact, Chita was barking at whatever was on the pavement and Janus was telling *her* to shut up. Just occasionally, they reversed roles, and she told him I was telling them to be quiet.

I never stopped the dogs barking in the car at first; they stopped on a signal later. I have twice had men open my passenger door when I have been parked in a layby having a sandwich, demanding a lift. The first time I hadn't a dog, but I did have to pass the police station and my unwanted passenger did not argue when two policemen came and removed him for me; the second time Puma was lying in the back and exploded as the door opened. I had no trouble whatever with that one. He went, fast.

My dogs are my protection, and the world isn't made up of saints.

So I let them bark at visitors at first, as they couldn't know which were friends and which were unwanted until I told them. No one would have heard me if I'd screamed alone here. I would never have stayed alone without the dogs.

Meanwhile, there was a difference between a sensible warning and constant yelling, and if Chita was to stay she had to learn. Trouble was, trying to teach her. She was so black determined to do her own thing that she refused to learn. She had by now learned I wouldn't have her pull me over; well, mostly. If she saw something that took her fancy, she lunged to the end of her lead – and she was extremely strong; so strong that at eighteen weeks old, she unbalanced a large police-dog handler, much to his amazement; not to mine. I had warned him, but she was such a scrap of nothing that he took no notice of me.

She was very small.

I worried about this till I met others from her stock. Both her grandfather on one side, and her father, produce small-built offspring; and I have now met a number all her size and some much smaller. I needn't have worried at all, but again it's a matter of finding out. Until you begin to travel to shows again and meet people all over the country, you just don't know; and often the people who breed don't know either, unless they too travel and ask a lot of questions.

Now, two years later, it is almost funny to remember the battles we had. Chita lies quiet; if she wants to go out, it is a restrained whimper. She may whine a bit while waiting impatiently to start a track, but the unearthly yells are a thing of the past. I hope I never have to live through the early days of another pup like her. I doubt if I could stand it over again.

She needed four meals a day. She needed to go out six times a day, at least; out into a wild autumn, an autumn of fierce gales and wicked icy winds, that I hated and she hated. She was always wind crazy; the wind seemed to make her almost uncontrollable. She also ran in frantic circles on the field on nights on which there was a full moon. I learned to take her out leashed at full moon.

She never wanted to settle; she never wanted to rest. She wanted to play and play and play, she wanted to play rough, and if put in her pen she circled it like a wild animal, a very odd light in her eyes. She yelled to be out, to be free, to be doing; but doing was always very destructive and couldn't be allowed. She'd already ruined two pairs of pigskin gloves, and eaten her way through five woollen gloves; if free, she climbed; to the chair, to the chair back, to the shelf. She ate a library book, which was very embarrassing; all that was left was the shiny yellow cover; that apparently did not taste too good. She climbed on my desk and chewed the knob on my typewriter. She fell out of the window and ran riot among the builders' rubble, careering off with one of Kenneth's favourite screwdrivers, losing it in the grass. It didn't improve his opinion of her. 'Your blasted pup,' became his theme song.

She ate pens, she ate pencils. She destroyed every dog toy we had. Janus and Puma had had them for years; allowed free, Chita stole them and chewed them into pieces. She had bones; bones weren't half so much fun.

I had 'flu, which didn't help at all, as I got a cough afterwards and felt wretched, but Kenneth couldn't cope with her. She just wouldn't go outside and perform for him. She had a weird little ritual. She would make a puddle quickly as soon as she got out; but before she could do anything else, she had to run to the edge of the wall and gaze over it into the field; then she'd stare at the sky, run back to the sycamore tree and look up at that. This she'd repeat about four times, and then she found herself a spot to empty, usually high on the bank, where she performed very thoughtfully, looking exactly like a kangaroo from the back. If the ritual was interrupted, we had to start right at the beginning again. Goodness knows what it did for her, but it did work; and on dark nights, at midnight, when the wind was screeching in the trees and the rain was coming down so hard that both of us loathed every second of our exodus, it did make her hurry if I started her off on her absurd little pattern.

People rang me; couldn't talk as Chita yelled. People came and their visits were not very rewarding. One or two came with dogs, which didn't help either, as I was trying to get Chita to understand that when dogs were not being trained or exercised they had to lie quite still and be sensible. They had plenty of free running time; if we were busy, or eating, or using the phone, dogs had to lie quiet. But other people's dogs often don't remain quiet either, and visiting us turned life into a minor hell, as they excited Chita till she was unbearable. If I were writing, dogs *had* to lie quiet; she was stopping me earning my living, and nothing I was writing now was any good; I was far too tired.

This little lunatic was impossible. I longed to discuss her with people who ought to be able to help.

I was writing about her for the Alsatian League magazine; pup's progress. It was a remarkably odd progress; progress more or less nil. I found writing for breeders a not very rewarding experience, as they have their own jargon and I have mine and it doesn't mean the same thing at times!

I found people read deeply something I hadn't intended to be taken deeply. I wrote on one occasion that I hadn't been concerned with Puma's early training. Someone took me to task: I *should* have been concerned.

But I was not concerned *with* her training; it wasn't my concern. I didn't take her home till she was nearly two; other people trained her. It's difficult when people use words differently, as they do in different parts of the country. I found when I went home to Kent last year that I had no problems in being understood. I was back where my rather odd sense of humour *was* understood; it came from there. And my accent was understood; they knew I was local, though it's a good many years since I left home. Home is the place you were born in, where you don't have to make an effort as the people around you are all like you. Elsewhere, you can be a total alien and never know why.

I took Chita visiting a long way away, back to my own patch, back to my old friends; friends who didn't mind a puppy visiting, who had dogs of their own, whom I could talk with and discuss this odd little morsel that had been wished on me. Friends who had pups from breeders I might have bought from; different breeding, far easier. I looked at them; pups that didn't scream, pups being trained for competition and already, at eight or nine months, under control. I doubted if Chita ever would be under control. I wasn't even sure at this stage that I would keep her, but I did know now that if I got rid of her, it would be a crime to re-settle her; no one else would enjoy her either. She would make as much mess of their lives as she was making of mine and the only answer would be death.

I took her over to a friend who trains police dogs and their handlers.

He took her from me, and started to show her what to do.

"Heel nicely, little girl, sweet little girl."

I watched, a little maliciously.

He is a very big man. She was a very small pup.

The next second, he yelled at her.

"We'll have some discipline, miss."

47

He gave her a lesson; he gave me a lesson. It wasn't the kind of lesson he had intended.

She was then fifteen weeks old.

I looked at her as I got in the car to go home and she glared at me. A moment later, as I put a hand out to the other two dogs, who always come for fussing, a small cold nose crept towards my wrist. It was the first contact she had made of her own free will. In that moment I knew I had to go on. The first link had been forged in a chain that now binds us.

Chapter Four

Although we lived at the end of nowhere, socialising the puppy was vital, so I made sure we went out every day and went away to stay with friends or family many weekends. For one thing, being away at weekends meant that Kenneth got some peace from the puppy. He definitely wasn't at all enthusiastic and, maddeningly, not being very dog-minded, he made matters worse by fussing the two older dogs and ignoring the baby, so that she felt left out, and I had to make up for it, which upset the two older dogs.

It was like going round and round the mulberry bush; we weren't getting anywhere much.

By the time she was sixteen weeks old she had demonstrated her paces to a Senior Citizens' group and I was rather surprised to find that in fact we had made progress. She decided for once to co-operate and trotted round on her lead, a minute scrap of self-importance. Chita was always very aware of her own personality and put it over wherever she was; not always as I would have wished.

She trotted at heel and she sat. She came up to everyone and she 'kiss kissed' which was an enormous relief as I wasn't at all sure she wouldn't 'bite bite', and I was taking a bit of a risk. She enjoyed being liked; she was fussed and petted and stroked and came back in the car behaving rather well for once. It was a break in our long hard haul.

She was learning to come when called; fine on the end of a long line, but otherwise not on your life. So she had little freedom, except on the long line. She couldn't be off lead as she could get through the hedge, which the older dogs couldn't; or she could get under the gate which the older dogs couldn't. And, much to our amazement, when I stayed with my friend Joy, who has two Shelties and a totally fenced-in garden, plus a gate with a very narrow gap under it, Chita managed to squeeze under that. She came out to me, as I stood by the car, preparing to drive it into the gap made by a visitor leaving with his car. Luckily, she was looking for me and didn't run off.

We stayed with Joy a number of times, starting very early on. Her two Shelties were remarkably tolerant of this intruder. They knew Janus and Puma well.

She visited shops that allowed her in; she visited bookshops. She came with me on a signing session and the children adored her and she behaved. Although she was only a baby she had to learn, as signing sessions were part of my life; and so were book shows. The older dogs were well used to those and knew the routine well.

They had come to two schools since we moved to Wales, lying at my feet while I talked; and if the children looked bored we did a small obedience routine. Chita would have to learn too, but I wasn't yet ready to take her anywhere too far away.

We had an invitation to Liverpool, to a book show in the crypt of the Roman Catholic Cathedral. She would be exactly eighteen weeks old; four and a half months.

She was fairly well house-trained, and puddled only if she was excited. She didn't yell quite so much; she had co-operated when we demonstrated to the Senior Citizens and again to the WI. She was beginning sometimes to walk to heel instead of diving off all the time; she did sometimes obey my voice.

There were a couple of weeks to go before we visited Liverpool. Time to get her more reliable. Time to write a couple of articles about her for the dog magazines that were interested in her. I had written about Janus and Puma. I had written about the right way to bring up a pup and a remarkable number of people were interested to find out how I was faring with this new one. This puppy that was to be brought up in the ideal way, trained in the ideal way, just as the books said. Just as I had been taught; just as I had learned from Janus and Puma, whom I'd bought as older dogs.

The Fates were screaming with laughter the day that Chita was born.

She would have been far easier to cope with if she had been horrible all the time; I would have given up quickly and got myself a dog from easier breeding; a dog that hadn't that amount of working stock in her ancestry, one that had been chosen because she was submissive. I had had several years of problems with a dominant golden retriever. A dominant German Shepherd was something else again.

But she wasn't always horrible; when she chose to co-operate she was endearingly sweet. One of my articles began: "Anyone who misunderstands this can put it down to Chita. I don't usually write articles with a puppy climbing me. Days go by and she is fuller and fuller of herself, sure we all adore her as she adores us."

She was also determined that Kenneth should adore her. She had decided he was not only the most wonderful creature in her life, but that as he bossed Janus and also me, he was her boss. This meant that she submitted to him. The only way she knew how to submit was by piddling on his feet, a puppy trait also seen in some older bitches. Some mares do the same thing. It doesn't matter in a stable.

This, in spite of her efforts, wasn't in the least calculated to impress him. It resulted in the complaint that he had never known a puppy before that caused him to want to live in Wellingtons, even indoors. Indoors we had, at that time, carpet tiles, which proved unsatisfactory on concrete floors. They slipped, so we replaced them later with fitted carpet. I seemed to spend a good deal of my life picking up the latest puddle and washing the tile under the tap and trying to dry it. It was a remarkably well-cleaned floor.

She never came, as the older dogs did, gently up to us, pushing a nose into our hands or leaning lovingly against us. Even when she needed love, she forced herself at us, trying to climb into our laps, washing noses and ears, licking at hands, her tail almost coming off with excitement. And with Kenneth, those few drops meant she had no intention of challenging him, which always managed to infuriate him, so that she undid all the good

51

she might have done by being totally unable to control her bladder. She never meant to do it, she could have been outside in the garden and made an enormous pool; it was quite impossible for her to control it. It worried her, and I knew she couldn't be punished for it, as little pups often wet themselves trying to show older dogs that they are not going to threaten them or offer themselves as challenger in the pack. Kenneth was obviously Pack Leader. Maybe it was under control and we couldn't make her understand *we* didn't need that kind of message. Dog language is very different from ours, and that leg cocked against a gate leaves a mass of information only intelligible to the canine race.

Chita never puddled for Janus; he wasn't her boss. She never puddled with me, even after she accepted my authority. Perhaps she only did it for men, as the vet was another person who provoked Chita to produce a pool; the nurses kept the tissues handy whenever she came for an injection. Her whole body wagged, from head to tail, and a puddle appeared. It seemed to mystify her. She'd look at it in amazement. Where did that come from?

One night Kenneth came in at two in the morning, having had to go south for a family funeral. I was asleep and woke to hear the dogs greet him. I was not at all pleased when he came upstairs and announced that my blasted pup had flooded the floor again. I could go down and mop it up.

The older dogs always took care to keep their distance, to prove they had nothing to do with this effort. Puma looked disapproving; Janus usually had a smug expression on his face. "I don't do that, do I?" his attitude seemed to say.

It was something that would be with Chita for a very long time; Kenneth learned to greet her outside. It was so much part of her that when we had a burst pipe one Christmas night, two years later, she worried in case I thought that an inch of water all over three floors could have been her doing. Neither of us could account in any other way for her servile behaviour throughout that day. I had found three dogs standing, howling, in a gathering flood, unable to attract our attention, as the walls are two feet thick and we all slept soundly.

Slowly, as Chita grew from sixteen to twenty weeks old, the dogs' attitude to her changed.

It was hard to remember Janus had loathed the puppy as he lay on the floor, Chita sprawled on his tummy, trying to 'eat' him, while he tried to 'eat' her. All three dogs spent a lot of time 'eating' one another.

The games indoors were followed by games outdoors. One shouldn't let a puppy run with older dogs, but no one who saw this one would try to stop her, as her idea of living was to carry on running. I nearly renamed her Perpetual Motion. I have never met any other dog that could do a vigorous sitstay, walking fast backwards on her front paws and her bottom, a totally idiotic grin on her face; or move at incredible speed round and round her pen. Even her dreams were vigorous and her legs moved as she slept, so did her tail.

Outdoors, her favourite game was to hide under Kenneth's trailer, while the big dogs pretended they couldn't see her. Out she'd bounce, squealing, and in they'd run, and pounce at her, so that she retreated under the trailer again and lay there, small pup hiding. Janus and Puma once more pretended she had gone, and off they went together, rolling and 'biting', running and jumping. They had always played a form of tag that Puma evolved when she discovered retrievers lumber, they don't glide over the ground the way a properly made German Shepherd does. Puma floated over the ground, her movement the most beautiful thing about her; Janus lurched after, his movement quite horrible, his bad hip thrown out the way a human with a hip disability lurches around. He was never aware of it, and ran contentedly on. But he could never catch Puma unless she let him, and let him she did, keeping him totally happy and convinced he had outrun her.

When she discovered pup had illusions about keeping up, she taught her a lesson, ran full out and puppy trotted after. This proved unprofitable, and she soon found a stick instead and proceeded to kill it. She carried anything she found, her favourite toy being a plastic flowerpot big enough to hide her funny little face; so that big dogs sat with mouths open, apparently roaring with laughter at the flowerpot prancing around on four legs.

The flowerpot had a number of drawbacks, as Chita couldn't see where she was going; but she was determined not to drop it, not even if she crashed headlong into the garage door. Determination, it soon became obvious, should have been her middle name, as nothing on earth made Chita give up an idea once she got it; and she got a good many. I had to be very forceful. No meant no.

A few nights before we went to Liverpool, she was lying on the hearthrug with her legs in the air, a favourite position. Her bone was in her mouth and she was juggling with it. It wasn't the easiest of positions in which to eat a bone.

Kenneth was watching television. I was half watching, and doing my accounts; a most unfavourite occupation, unfortunately demanded by Her Majesty's Government from the self-employed.

Chita rolled over and looked at me earnestly. She went on looking. She was now showing signs of being more or less the same colour as Puma, but with a much darker face; her eyes were still minute boot buttons, and oddly round. Puma's eyes were atypical; large and soulful, which isn't usual for her breed, but she had most compelling eyes that talked to you, and gave her a lovely kind expression. Chita's just gave her a rather odd expression. She was far from being a pretty puppy, but I consoled myself with the fact that pretty babies are rarely beautiful when adult; and pretty pups often make ugly adults. I was right to console myself, as the prettiest puppy I ever saw grew into a rather odd looking grown bitch, and the ugly puppy I had became extremely pretty, her weird little eyes changing completely to mid-brown almonds, centred with black, giving her an extremely old-fashioned expression on occasions.

She went on staring at me.

"What on earth do you imagine that puppy is thinking?" I asked Kenneth, and the next moment I knew, as with all the forcefulness in her power, and even at that age there was a good deal, she leaped at me, jumping into my lap and shoved her bone into my mouth.

It tasted disgusting.

I appreciated the thought. "Poor Mistress; no bone. She can share mine." Neither Puma nor Janus ever dreamed of letting me share their bones, though I could take them away from them whenever I chose as I never allowed protectiveness. Chita had been taught to give me her bone when I asked.

Now I hadn't asked and I had got it. I tried to push her off and got the bone instead in my ear.

I managed to persuade her that people eat bones with their fingers. I didn't mind holding it; no way was I going to gnaw it! At last she did get the idea; it had been quite a fight. Now she stood and chewed one end while my hand 'chewed' the other end, and this is something she has continued to do all her life.

Gnawing a bone, she suddenly realised I was sitting there without one, and over she came, as always full of firm determination, and thrust it hard into my hand. "You have a go." Very few dogs share their bones with their owners, so I never refused. I accepted the honour in the spirit her small dog mind meant it, and we spent a happy half hour, during which she blissfully chewed away, and I got extremely bored.

At this stage, she was still apt to grab my hand when she greeted me; she no longer bit, but her teeth hurt and I got bruised. I discovered that if I squealed as she grabbed me, she became extremely anxious. "Did I hurt? Oooh, sorry," and I would promptly be showered with kisses, as all her life Chita has been a born enthusiast. Even when she got things wrong, she did that too with a great deal of showiness, being wronger than any dog I ever met, but quite unable to make out why or to change her ways easily.

Everything round the house and outside it fascinated

her, including the rainpools on the uneven concrete path, which she insisted on drinking, and with occasionally dire results, as they weren't always just water. The builders dropped putty and various other things around. She also, from the day I got her, drank to excess. She drank so much I thought there was something wrong with her kidneys, as she had three full bowls of water daily; it worried me immensely, as Puma drank one and Janus only half a bowl. Breeds do vary, but this tiny mite was bloated with water.

It rectified slowly when I changed her food, but it was over six months before she relaxed and drank what seemed to me a normal amount. Wherever I went with Chita I had a big polythene container and she had a drink every time I stopped the car. The older dogs refused. Needless to say all that water had to go somewhere, so journeys when Chita was small were very stop and go again, and meetings with Kenneth were fraught with puddly hazards.

At this stage she became a bit more co-operative; a puppy trying to please. She often got it wrong, as she always wanted to be first. First to be fed, first in the car, first out; first through the door, first to greet me in the morning. Me, me, me, was Chita's constant cry. Blow other dogs. Blow big dogs. *Me*.

It wasn't always possible to stop her racing out of the door, and refusing to come in, no matter how hard I tried. She could slip through the smallest gap; or between my legs, or under the other dogs. I evolved a new system: dogs out, biscuits on the porch windowsill; whistle and hold up a biscuit. No need to ask who was first one home, it was always Chita.

Then Janus had a brainwave.

Out, cock his leg, do nothing whatever (well, it was what I wanted, wasn't it) and come in again for his biscuit. Puma copied; squat for one second and get there before puppy, who had to perform as her holding-on powers weren't very good.

So I had to go up the field with them and insist they

performed, which did us all good as now everybody will go on command; very useful when about to set off on a journey, or when we broke one. Out, say "Hurry up, be clean" and they were. I had a visit from someone with a nine-week-old golden retriever puppy who came to join the dog club later and never turned up! They saw my dogs. Chita jumped; Janus came out and showed them how nicely he walked on lead. Puma hadn't been out that morning so, before I did anything with her, I took her on the field on her lead, as she is apt to bark at visitors and these had a six-year-old with them. I said "Hurry up, then, girl," and she squatted and did. That was one thing that really did impress them and make them feel maybe I could train dogs!

Chita continued to be faster than lightning; in no time at all she too was in for her biscuit, having taken several short cuts that were definitely rather dangerous. Down the bank and jump the wall. Puppies aren't supposed to jump. Puppies aren't supposed to run fast; they aren't supposed to have a lot of exercise.

Puppies are supposed to sleep a lot. It was no use trying to tell Chita. The only way to stop her running non-stop was to pen her, even when she was too big to pen. Luckily her pen had become her den. I fed her in it, as that prevented older dogs stealing her food and that she would not have tolerated. They had to have their food cut back and a biscuit every time she was fed, as she was on three meals a day to their one. She refused to go to sleep unless her pen enclosed her safely.

The older dogs had to be dieted or they got fat. I gave Chita all she could take, plus bread and butter, plus sunflower oil, plus anything extra I could think of; rice pudding, custard, all the things that fattened me. She could eat them without harm, but put on weight? Not she.

She had also found several new hobbies. For weeks, friends of mine were regaled with letters in envelopes decorated with puppy teeth marks; I have never discovered quite what she did to an outsize reel of Sellotape that never did look the same again, or even peel off after a Chita session. Paper tissues turned into confetti; logs were carried all round the hall, pinched from the log basket.

Then we got a Chita-proof box – or so we thought. It was proof against the other two, but Chita could open it. It never occurred to the others to lift the lid and take out the contents. It did to Chita. She also became the only dog in the house to depress the handle. Her teeth pulled the door open, or else she pushed.

I needed to train her to walk properly on the lead if we were to go to Liverpool. Chita hadn't heard about walking nicely all the time either; she still made sorties after anything that took her fancy; moving in small dives. Dash after cat, dash after bird (never mind that it's seventy feet up in the air), dash after the helicopter, which is also high above her. Dash after anything that moves, or that smells. My arm began to ache. I remembered that from Janus. That particular pain had been dormant for six years. Now here we went again. I remembered everything I had been taught; I read more books. Chita went right on pulling to the top of her strength and it was a lot of strength for a young puppy.

Let Chita do as Chita wanted and Chita was adorable. I thought of the nursery rhyme:
'There was a little girl who had a little curl right in the middle of her forehead;
When she was good she was very very good but when she was bad she was horrid.'
Chita was only happy so long as I never made her behave properly!

Since she was an extremely inventive puppy, with apparently more brains than most, and since all her inventions led to ultimate disaster for either her or me or one of the other dogs, she had to be curbed. And curbed, she behaved abominably. . .

Gentle sweet puppy. Gentle sweet hellcat, fighting the lead, fighting authority, fighting Puma, who at this stage simply took the pup's head in her mouth and forced it down against the ground. Later, Chita was too strong to restrain and pushed Puma's head down, which did nothing for Puma's morale.

Then she tried fighting Janus, who roared at her like a bull, baring his teeth. "Behave, little horror." Little horror did. One day in the car when she had screamed at everyone she saw (people weren't allowed to walk anywhere near Chita's car, or stand at the traffic lights or cross pedestrian crossings if we were waiting), I said to Janus, "Oh, for heaven's sake, tell her off."

I didn't expect him to understand. Possibly his patience had been frayed as much as mine, as Chita had a most unpleasant bark, high pitched and sounding mildly insane. It was agonising in the confinement of the car. People were petrified by it where they could take Puma's deeper bay. Janus had a very deep bark too; this unpleasant cross between a wild cat and an air-raid siren took all our patience.

Janus roared.

I had never heard him make such a noise. Puma landed in the front passenger seat and cowered; puppy actually shut up and I nearly hit a bus. It had been a ridiculous thing to do; I hadn't expected any result. It was something I would never do again in the car, but it had its effect. Chita did shut up.

She wasn't cowed. Nothing cows her. I suspected she could be beaten and still not bother; she seemed totally insensitive to pain and, where most dogs would be yelling at the vet, she had a cut on her paw dressed without any fuss, and a thorn that invaded a pad and went septic didn't bother her until it was really very bad indeed. She did complain a little the night the paw suddenly swelled like a balloon and it hurt her to walk on it. Janus and Puma would have been demented with pain at that point and would have complained long before she did.

She had had a little training and she did respond in some ways; she sat on the X-ray table without moving, while the picture of her paw was taken. She didn't even budge when the thing 'zzzzed' at her. She put her head on one side, curious. She waited patiently while it was developed. She did four-minute standstays at home for the next week without moving, her hind paw soaking in a bowl of warm Epsom salts, to remove the poison; and stood meekly till I produced a towel and took her paw to prevent floods on the floor. She sat in front of me for her pill and took it without the slightest fuss. She was beginning also to want praise, where before, she had shown no sign of knowing the difference between praise and scolding. She was a very odd puppy indeed.

People seeing her for a short while obviously thought I was inventing. She acted quite normally as long as we were on home ground. It was outside that the trouble started; not with people but with dogs. There was no room in Chita's world for any dog that didn't belong to her pack. In the wild, she would have been a killer, boss of all the packs; that is, unless she met one equal to her, and at the time Janus was more than equal; no dog or bitch defied Janus. He wouldn't tolerate it, and few people realise how much he had to be controlled. He was attacked twice when only a young pup, and dogs remember. If any dog curled a lip at Janus, Janus would go right in at once. But when leashed and under command, he knew that when I said "sit," I meant it. And he sat till the dog went. A dog can't fight a sitting target; it doesn't have the right reactions, and everything a dog does depends on signals from the other dog.

I had had a lot of practice with Janus. I needed it with this one.

She didn't mind Janus disciplining her. She took it and behaved. He was a great help in keeping her under some sort of control. The story that dog never disciplines bitch is not true. I've seen it happen a number of times. Puma has twice been bitten by a dog, not a bitch, and she didn't even retaliate.

Chita's idea of fun was to race out of the house, up the field, rush at people coming in the gate, leaping high to kiss, not to bite. It was progress, but few people who see a half-grown German Shepherd coming full tilt are quite confident that it won't bite when it arrives. It is very alarming. Children are terrified so she must learn to behave.

Some of the smaller breeds are in fact much more deadly under these circumstances but they don't look it, so the German Shepherd, doing its job of guarding, gets a bad name. The only thing to do with Chita was make sure she didn't go outside, even on our own property, except on the lead. Which she didn't like, so she fought it.

We can't see the gate from the house and, not being telepathic, I never know who is coming down; it could be someone collecting for Lifeboats, or Poppy Day, or the man to read the meter; they could be terrified of dogs. So Chita had to learn, and if she wouldn't learn the easy way it had to be the other way; by sheer domination on my part.

Before I had this puppy I would never have dreamed that a young dog could be such a nightmare; and she *was* a nightmare. But the trouble was that when she wasn't fighting, she was adorable. It would have been so easy if she hadn't been. Never mind, she would improve as she matured; she couldn't get worse, could she?

She could, and she did as she grew stronger. Leaped higher and was determined everyone needed their faces washing, so she tried on every occasion. I had reservations about taking her to the Liverpool Book Show. She would be in public and there were to be about a thousand children there. She was still small enough to pick up if she was naughty; it would be like holding an eel but it was just possible. Maybe she would turn over a new leaf. I have always been an optimist, which is perhaps just as well.

Liverpool never was my favourite city to drive in. It was a grey day, a dull day, and the motorway as always was full of heavy lorries belting along at speeds that seemed lethal to anything smaller. I never have liked motorway driving at all.

We had to go through the tunnel and I hate tunnels, as when we were children en route to my grandparents for lunch, we had to go through one of the tunnels under the

Thames. One Christmas, some idiot had a bright idea and tried to overtake, causing himself to form the middle of a sandwich. We spent most of that Christmas Day in Blackwall Tunnel. I can think of far better places, and have been nervous underground ever since. Tunnels still, too!

I had to find the Cathedral. Liverpool had seen fit to change its one-way system. I could see the Cathedral, it was difficult not to, but I felt like Alice in Wonderland, who found things disappearing as she reached them and had to start again. At last I gave up, and fished out my Presscard (I am a member of the Institute of Journalists). I found a taxi driver and showed it to him and told him I was to sign books at 11.00 am. It was then 10.30am. Could he guide me there and I would pay as if I had been his fare?

He guided me to the wrong side of the Cathedral, though neither of us knew that. I arrived on a piece of waste ground, beside a shelter for alcoholics and others in distress. I locked the car and went to find the main entrance, where one of the Cathedral Fathers was waiting for me. I suspect he expected someone rather like Barbara Cartland, very grand and all dressed up; and here was this tiny person in trousers and blazer instead. He was very kind and came with me to show me how to get into the Cathedral underground car park.

He was rather flummoxed to find a car with three dogs in it.

I exercised the dogs on the waste ground, which caused a certain number of problems, as Chita as usual had her own ideas about correct behaviour and managed to create chaos. We drove halfway round the one-way system to get to the other side of the Cathedral, and in we went.

The car park is right under the Cathedral so I put the three dogs on their leads and went upstairs; two big dogs excited and interested, but behaving well, and pup busily doing her own thing, which involved pulling, sniffing, and generally making life extremely difficult for me. At that stage, she was very like one of our recent club dogs, a for more delightful pup than she, but in his early days he too had the conviction that he was a cross between a yo-yo and a vacuum cleaner. Co-operation was not in her mind.

Nobody seemed to know we were there or why we were there and I couldn't remember which of my publishers had invited me, but very soon my paperback publishers realised I was there, and from then on we were extremely busy, signing books so fast my hand began to ache. We had an idiotic problem as some nut had advertised me as Joyce Stranger and her Performing Dogs. Enthusiasm, sometimes, can be very misguided. Chita, however, was determined to perform, though her performance was certainly not what the posters had led the children to expect. They adored her so it didn't matter.

She enjoyed the children and they enjoyed her. For once, I had an angelic puppy-like puppy and not a fiend in a fur coat. There were no other dogs there, which helped. Janus and Puma by now were part of her family and she accepted them and obeyed them if they insisted, which Janus always did and Puma rarely. Puma was very much an anything-for-a-quiet-life type.

There were monsters: large pantomime animals prancing around, a giant kangaroo, a 'Thing' from Dr Who, a massive Snoopy, apparently ballet-trained and doing little pas-de-deux all over the place, rather oddly. Puma had never seen monsters before. She retired behind the chair and looked so haunted that at twelve o'clock I decided to put her back in the car. Taking her back meant finding my guide to unlock all the doors, and of course taking all three dogs with me.

The underground car park was cool; no one was there except us, so I could open all the windows part way and Puma could rest safely in the dark. She would be happier than in a milling crowd and it wouldn't be for long.

Back we went, this time just puppy and Janus. There were things going on; there were children everywhere, and a slippery floor, and more monsters. There was an echo, and Janus was so overcome by it all he barked.

A dog barked back at him.

He stared at me in amazement.

"Funny, that bark sounded like my bark. Couldn't be, could it?" His eyes were eloquent.

"Shhh," I said.

He shhhed, but he was thinking. Janus often thought to odd purpose. We'd lose him in the evening sometimes and find him sitting in front of the bread bin, a pool of saliva on the floor, thinking about bread. It might just pop out of the bin into his mouth, perhaps? Or he could be thinking about the car and suddenly appear with my purse, a preliminary to any outing. He thought; and he barked again, and again.

I quieted him, between signing books and telling children about Chita. Children were racing everywhere, were skating over the floor, were having a whale of a time. By the look on their faces, all the adults felt as I did and were rapidly developing headaches. Janus barked again, and That Dog barked back at him, so he replied.

By lunchtime, I had had enough of him too. Nothing would stop a sudden deep bark, then an amazed expression as he heard the reply from the invisible dog. Or did he know it was his own voice?

Our poor guide once more led us through all the locked doors to the car; he would have to lead me back after lunch to get the dogs out, and again when I left, and it was a long way. Dogs safely in the car, I was shown round the Cathedral, which is beautiful. Very modern and nothing like any cathedral I had seen before, and I know Canterbury, York, Lincoln, Bangor, Hereford, and the London cathedrals.

We lunched at a vegetarian bistro on quite the ghastliest food I have ever been served. I had a sort of red bean curry, which wasn't edible at all. I ate one mouthful. Yuk! The pudding was edible. I went back feeling slightly sick and rather hungry, and with a now well-established thumping headache.

Meanwhile, I couldn't face Janus barking any more so left him with Puma. The back of the car was roomier than moot kennels, they had plenty of air and water and I gave them each a small meal; not too much, as we were travelling.

Back to the main hall with Chita. She was restless, and I walked her round the hall. She saw the giant kangaroo and began to stalk its tail, pouncing as it swung. It was a gorgeous game, but might end in the tail coming off, so we shifted our ground, straight into one of the bug-eyed monsters from space, immense and bright green.

"Hallo, puppy," it said, and bent to stroke her.

She responded to the human voice; it smelled human, anyway. She stood against the creature, on her hind legs, small ears pricked, eyes bright with interest, a tiny black and gold puppy, dwarfed by this immense pantomime beast, quite unafraid, accepting this as yet another part of a world that constantly produced astonishment.

There were boxes that sang or talked or made pictures; dragons on wheels that roared and bellowed, and in which puppies could travel; enormous rooms full of people who thought a puppy was lovely. She revelled in it and I wished I had a camera to record the idiotic sight.

Everyone laughed at her and she obviously thought it all fun. Her small otter tail, which even at two had remained an otter tail, almost devoid of the dense fur that Puma boasted, was weaving wildly and in quite undignified fashion. Dignity was something else that Chita would never achieve.

She was a hellcat all right, but boy, was she a character!

I drove home, knowing that somehow, I didn't know how, I was going to civilise her. I had bought her intending to do Obedience and Working Trials, and she would do them or we'd both come to grief in the attempt. I had a challenge; a dickens of a challenge, and I wasn't going to give up.

I had a further slight challenge in that Liverpool doesn't signpost its tunnel very well and apparently both tunnels had vanished. It was rush hour, not the time to be dithering about finding your way. I knew the way home from Runcorn, and I knew how to get to Runcorn; all around the moon to go back to Wales, but at least it would be safer than trying to dodge around in this lot.

I stopped to exercise the dogs and eat at a Little Chef; a vast improvement on my meal of red beans. We got home very late and Chita actually slept on the way home.

One thing, I had no fears about her as long as no other dogs were about, and I felt I could accept future invitations among children without trepidation.

There was another invitation waiting for me when I got home, this time to a school in Liverpool that was putting on its own book show. The letter came from the Charles Wilson bookshop, in Liverpool itself.

Visits to book shows made a change from writing. I wasn't competing in dog events as yet. The older dogs were retiring, pup not ready.

Book shows gave me a different occupation, a change of scene and new people to meet, socialising me as well as the puppy. I needed them, as I no longer enjoyed dog class.

Walking down our lane one morning, a village collie bit Chita badly under the chin; a messy sort of bite that took months to heal as it started up a form of acne. And Chita, who had never much liked any dogs but her own home pack of Puma and Janus, decided, every time we met a dog anywhere, dog club, dog show, vet, beach, forest, or in the village, she would kill it. And no way was she going up the lane in case that dog was there. She sat mutinous, at our gate. "Won't move. Won't ever go down there again." Every muscle was tense. Her expression was eloquent, her ruff bristled.

She came in the car, though if we saw the collie that had bitten her we all needed ear muffs and Janus joined in, apparently aware that this creature had caused trouble. The dog ran free, and his idea of fun was to leap at the back of my parked car, barking at my dogs. People wondered why my dogs barked at other dogs; and this was a daily occurrence, as I had to stop in the village to pick up food and my newspaper, to bring down the milk, to post letters. There was no way I could prevent the daily exchange of insults.

He also chased my car and one day, as he ran in front of me and I braked and all my dogs fell over, I lost my temper, and leaped out. I brandished the lead, yelling, "I'll kill you, you idiot," and watched with satisfaction while he took to flight down the road. Unfortunately, he is only afraid of me when I am there, and I can't be by my car and in the shop.

Meanwhile, I had to cure Chita of raving at every dog she met; out to the end of the lead and scream, "I'll kill you before you kill me." Hair on end, back bristling, looking totally evil with an odd wild light in her eyes that was quite extraordinary.

Also, I had to get her down the lane again on her paws, not in the car. She couldn't be allowed to develop a hang-up about our only exit to the world, and I didn't always want to be in the car.

But how did I cure her of both problems?

At home, like all dogs, she was beginning to co-operate; but with any distraction, however small, she was totally impossible, and I began to think I would never train her. If only, somewhere, there was someone who knew more than I did. There were a great many people who knew far less; a great many people who told me what to do, but were talking absolute nonsense because they didn't know my dog. They only knew their own.

And I was so tired, trying to get her under control and always having to fight her.

Chapter Five

Once more, I rang John Cree. He suggested coupling her to Janus when we went up the lane, Janus on one side of her and me on the other, so that she had total protection. This did work. Janus made the growling noises, I told dogs that ran up to us "No." Heaven knows what the village thought; probably that all writers were definitely mad! Intruding dogs did usually understand 'no', and we all relaxed again, until at last I could bring her up the lane on her own.

Once more she told every dog we met that she would kill it before it killed her. People looking at her didn't like her at all as she looked downright vicious, and if she had attacked would probably have been so; and no way could I take a dog like that to shows. I had never had trouble like this with any dog I had owned before. Janus had only attacked the breeds that attacked him first, and he soon learned not to do so.

This pup was bent on showing me that I knew nothing about dogs, which was very humiliating. You can cope with things you have had before, but not only had it not met this trait, no one else I knew had met it. I didn't know if it came from being bitten, or if it came from her breeding. I didn't know what the rest of the litter was like.

Meanwhile I had to do something about this attacking.

I tried sitting in the vet's and checking her every time a dog came in, which was exhausting, time-consuming and unrewarding, as people didn't like us and some dogs were ill and she might pick up a bug anyway. I tried walking her on the beach; other dogs had no right there according to Chita, and owners didn't like her.

I rang Ian, who is police sergeant in charge of Force dog training, and told him. "Bring her over," he said, and over we went, invited to lunch, to do some tracking and training with the off-duty dogs, and to try and cure Chita of raving at other dogs. We'd already been over, once – she was much worse now, in spite of all my efforts. We'd also been to the police near us.

Out came four dog handlers and four dogs and Chita. Chita yelled at them. They were all fully trained police dogs and told to leave her alone. They did, though plainly they felt she ought to be told off. We put my three in the police van, complete with their rugs, to persuade them to settle down, even though it caused amusement; they weren't used to being carried behind wire grills, on slippery metal. They did settle down and off we went into the wilds . . . which was just as well.

The older dogs were walked on lead; I walked Chita and she yelled at them. I checked her, and after about an hour (and a very exhausting hour) she deigned to relax, just a little. "Let her off," said Ian. I did. She went straight in to attack the biggest of the police dogs and she meant it. She raved at the top of her voice, hackles up, a miniature ball of nothing beside the fully-grown mature dogs. They looked most embarrassed. She continued to attack him until she was leashed. She was remarkably hard to catch.

Ian decided we would give her a mini track before lunch. I had recently had a present of a gorgeous leather tracking harness for her from a friend. It was far too large, but she would grow. Ian laid the track and she followed it well; she could track. She had just finished when he said, "Don't look now, but I think that cow's a bull!"

It was.

It was coming towards us slowly, suspiciously, head down, making puffing noises that sounded most alarming, as if it were getting up steam to charge. Ian gallantly shoved me towards the hedge, helped me hoist myself over, more or less threw Chita over, and came over himself just as the bull decided it would run.

We stood in the lane, breathing fast, and went off to lunch.

"What is Joyce's new dog like?" the Chief Superintendent asked in the middle of one of the excellent meals they always put on there.

Ian didn't have to think. "If Joyce will forgive me for telling the truth," he said, "She's an utter little swine!"

We went back to the kennels; out came one dog after another and, by the end of an exhausting afternoon, she was walking past them without raving at them, looking almost normal. One of the handlers took her. Without other dogs, she behaved moderately well; with them, she was little short of a nightmare.

She wasn't yet six months old. Obviously she needed a great deal of socialisation with other dogs. There was never the slightest problem with people. The question was how to find dogs regularly.

A friend suggested we hire the little village hall on Friday nights, and train our own dogs there; myself, she and her daughter. Both of them had worked dogs in Working Trials for years, one had owned a champion collie that was trained (by her) to do police work; the first collie in the country to get the Police Dog excellent qualification. They could help with Chita and they were experienced with dogs.

So, Friday after Friday, we went down till Chita learned that Simba and Shadow would not hurt her. Simba was a Flatcoat Retriever, lovely and bouncy, and Shadow a big fairly solemn German Shepherd that treated the pup kindly.

People learned we were working there and joined us, which proved a wonderful help, as Chita began to accept other dogs: four more German Shepherds came and a few other breeds; a spaniel and several cross-breeds. I went on socialising her.

I entered Janus in shows, not that it was much use as he simply wasn't getting the training necessary for show work; this little menace took all the time I had and more.

Just as I thought she was cured of raving at other dogs, it started again. She never did actually bite; she was still very young and by now I had met two people who had cured dogs of this behaviour, so maybe I could too.

Our vet, visiting once when Puma was ill, watched

70

Chita in amazement and said he'd never seen any pup so restless in his life. She would remain in her bed when we were alone, but the mere presence of a visitor excited her so that it was almost impossible for her to relax. She was also more excitable than any pup I had ever known. She could never stay in the car once we arrived at any destination; her paws scrabbled frenziedly at the window to get out, and she screamed. The only way to prevent her killing herself by racing into the road was to chain her in her crate, as no way was Chita going to learn to stay in the car. If the big dogs got in first, she screamed to be in with them; if they got out first, she screamed to join them. If she were thwarted, as they came out, she attacked them. Janus tossed her, and Puma took to either running indoors, if the door was open, or back into the car, or to lean against me.

"For Pete's sake, keep her away from me." Puma couldn't bear the din or the attack.

Janus had his own method of dealing with her. If she annoyed him, which she frequently did as she was a horrible little bully, he went off down the field. This invariably surprised the pup, who stood and watched with interest as he got up steam, rather like a bull. He was very solid and, being elderly, was now massive on the shoulders.

Down the field came Janus, head down, while pup watched.

"What's he up to?"

She soon found out, yet somehow she never learned (at times I think she is incapable of learning anything) that when he reached her, his head would go under her tummy, his shoulders hunch and up she would go in the air to land with a thud on the ground. It didn't worry her in the slightest; she seemed not to feel any pain.

Whatever Chita chose to do invariably caused trouble, as she had always to win. One of the favourite toys was the dog-pull. It was a rubber figure of eight that we had had for about six years; the two older dogs each took an end and pulled in a tug of war which neither ever won. Chita wanted to join in; she took it off them and bit right through it, something they had never managed.

Then Janus took his side and she pulled against Janus. He pulled her over the field, she giving way with great reluctance till, one day, I noticed he was having to make a great deal more effort than usual. Presently he dropped to the ground, unable to resist her but not ever allowing her to pull him forwards.

Next morning when the pull was on the field and Chita got it, Janus tried to take it off her. He had to drop again, but this time she dragged him an inch forwards; he dropped the pull, went off down the field and, as he lumbered towards her, he produced the most appalling roar of anger. I grabbed the pull and hid it under my jacket; tossed, Chita behaved again, and Janus soon seemed to forget he had to exert far more strength and authority. Puma might be bottom dog but no way was Janus going to allow Chita to be top dog. And I didn't want her there as she was battling with me, wanting to dominate me too; I had never met anything so dominant. So, sadly, the dog-pull had to be confiscated, and I only allowed its use if Chita were shut away in the house and the two other dogs were alone.

Chita was learning that in the house, if I said 'down', she went down. If she didn't, I held her down. I needed all my strength to do so, but I was not going to let this little beast get on top of me. No way. That lent me strength I didn't know I had.

I needed more than ever to meet someone who knew a lot about dogs of all types; someone who re-trained problem dogs for preference, as it was now plain that few of the pet clubs in the country had anyone who had the knowledge to start me on the right track with this particular animal.

I met people with easy dogs of her breed. I watched people who had lovely-tempered dogs of her breed. The four that came to club were all like Puma; charming and friendly with people and dogs. None was related to Chita.

I wrote to someone who had pups of similar breeding.

She replied that they were exhausting and singularly unrewarding. They had a different father but very similar bloodlines.

It wasn't me; if it were, Janus and Puma would both be awful with other dogs and they weren't. Janus would stand up to a dog that attacked him; Puma expected all dogs to be her very best friend and was terribly hurt when they weren't. She'd come to me with a sigh. "Did you see? I want to be friends; he doesn't. Want to be stroked," and she'd lean against me, at least secure in knowing that I was always there to comfort her when things go wrong.

I was still battling with Chita's hatred of other dogs when we had to go to a school in Liverpool. It was a grey wintry day and there was a lot of traffic. I walked all three dogs in a field before we got to the tunnel. It was only about twelve more miles to the school and we could relax once we were there, as they had told me on the phone there was a large patch of waste ground at the end of the school playground where I could exercise the dogs without worrying about children walking there.

Chita had done all a dog should in the field, but either she hadn't done it thoroughly or she didn't like the tunnel. Once we got into it, she decided to scream. Nothing would shut her up. I shouted, Janus roared, Chita yelled louder and louder. I closed the windows completely, hoping other cars couldn't hear her above the engine noises. I could; it was totally deafening and, since the tunnel was as claustrophobic as usual and my writer's imagination invariably started visualising hair-raising situations which would maroon us there, the thought of being marooned with a screeching banshee was quite demoralising. It was also hard to concentrate on where we were going, especially when I needed to find the right lane on exit.

It wasn't the tunnel upsetting her. She sounded as if she thought she was about to burst but, since there was absolutely nowhere to stop in the city traffic, she would have to burst. Her cage was well padded with newspaper just in case; and it wouldn't matter to me, although it would to Chita, as she was remarkably clean so long as she didn't get excited.

Kenneth still had to avoid greeting her, or she flooded the floor. It seemed she wasn't going to grow out of it. I'd thought it was puppy behaviour but she was now coming near to her first menstruation and her first season. It obviously worried her; it was one more annoying thing about Chita.

Now she needed out and she wasn't going to shut up till she'd been out.

At traffic lights, lorry drivers leaned out of their cabs and peered down to see if I really was killing a pig. When they saw the source of the din they grinned, as it was unbelievable that so much noise could come from anything so tiny. One man waved to me, thumb pointing upwards, unbelievably amused. It was deafening.

Luckily there was a grass verge before we reached the school. She did need to puddle again. We arrived in blissful silence and I just sat, before driving in to take the inevitable hurly burly of excited children, as we were to be there all day.

Chita behaved like an angel.

Nobody would believe she could be so evil. The children adored her. Puma came out of the car but, because of her failing sight, she became very anxious and I decided she would have to retire. She could stand people directly in front of her, but when they came fast from the side, she became more and more worried; plainly she needed consideration so she stayed in the car. Janus, who loves an audience, took it in turns to come out; first he, then Chita. Luckily it seemed to tire her to have children fussing her, and when she went into the car she slept and didn't yell. She had early cataracts, but was also very shortsighted. Dogs can't wear glasses! The day went off well; maybe I could do something with her after all. Maybe Chita would grow out of her fear of other dogs and her demoniacal behaviour when she met them. Maybe; you never know with dogs.

Once more we lost the tunnel signs and went the long

way round. Liverpool in the rush hour didn't appeal to me much anyway and I could unwind driving home; I could stop for a meal and, with three tired dogs in the car, I could drive in blissful silence. Just for once, the radio produced nice noises instead of idiotic ones, and the announcer was adult and didn't talk as if his audience all needed humouring and patting on the head, or make ghastly school-boy jokes that make the hearer wince. It had been a good day; a rare day.

Chapter Six

It was time to train Chita much more seriously. Up to now it had been puppy-play training. Advanced training proved to be something Chita did not like, as obeying anyone or anything but her own whims and inclinations was entirely foreign to her nature.

Like many dog owners, I am not exactly mad about puppies. They look very sweet; they can be very sweet, but they are wild dogs in need of calming and of training, and it's a long slow haul. Many people ignore the need to teach the baby how to behave, thinking it will come naturally, or it will grow to their ways. They never realise training and control starts with the baby and must be enforced to make the pup a social asset.

It only behaves if made to. Many people come to dog club convinced the trainer will wave a magic wand and, hey presto, the dog will be transformed from a devil to an angel; or else that the trainer will take the dog and do it all for them. Some, once they find out they have to do the work and that it *is* work, and moreover is *specialised* work, as it is a major skill to train a dog, just don't come back. Later the dog is put down as out of control.

Of course it is, as no one ever controlled it. But with someone who bothers to train the dog, nine out of ten will be safe and sensible. They *must* be *taught*.

It was very plain indeed to me that unless I taught Chita her manners and insisted, *she* would have to be put down as totally impossible. I had tried to show her nicely how a good puppy behaved. She didn't want to know.

She thought up the most idiotic ways of misbehaving. She ran along the windowsill, barking at the workmen. She strewed the contents of the wastepaper basket all over the floor. She tormented the cats who loathed her. People just looked at me when I described her latest escapade, apparently sure I was inventing. No one, however inventive, could invent half the things Chita did. Everything she met, anywhere, had to be inspected, tasted, and found out about. The basis of her finding out was 'is it edible?', and sometimes the result of her experiments came through and I found myself faced with a puppy with the oddest symptoms. The bright red 'blood' spots proved to be the berries off artificial holly. Several days of brilliant blue efforts proved to be a cache of blue silk squares I used for scent cloths for Janus; she had discovered them and managed to open the drawer and get them out, as apparently they tasted nice. I couldn't make out where she found them as she closed the drawer after removing the day's trophy. I was for ever saying no, and shaking her.

I had furniture in the oddest positions to guard the electric flexes, especially the leads to the TV set. She looked at TV, the others ignored it. It fascinated Chita, and she was the only one of the dogs that discovered that doorbells and phone ring on TV, and that when they did they could be ignored. A chiming doorbell in a TV serial sent Janus and Puma bellowing to the door; Chita lay there, looking superior. "It's only on TV, you nuts."

Luckily she did learn fast to bring me anything she picked up. I taught her to give and never said 'drop it', so that I knew what she had. Later, if I wanted to teach her to retrieve, the basis would be there. It wasn't always a welcome present that she brought me; one thing, she learned that if she brought things to me they must not be chewed, and also that, no matter what, for some odd reason I wanted it – everything she found.

Her offerings consisted of my purse, of gloves, now unchewed, which she still stole by climbing on to chairs and then shelves, apparently copying the cats; she brought me a ball of putty, which was as well as I gave her milk and she was soon sick; got rid of that.

She brought me a nice soft present which proved to be a fox-dropping; it stank to high heaven and I couldn't bear to eat even bread with my fingers for a week. Not that the smell really clung, but I felt as if it did. She brought

77

me a dead mouse that one of the cats had brought in.

She discovered the builders had dug a trench. It was not a very good idea to have a puppy belting hell for leather along an open trench leading to a septic tank suddenly found to be in need of renovation, and dug up and left open as the men didn't discover till they had dug it up that they couldn't buy the right sized pipes; there was a waiting list.

I discouraged her from licking paint; from drinking turpentine; (workmen are very casual and not really concerned about people's zany pups). She sampled dirty water used for mixing concrete. I tied her to the fence one day to keep her out of mischief while I gardened, heard a yell and discovered she had dug a large hole and was hanging by her collar over a four-foot drop on the other side of the fence. Janus and Puma had both been tied to that fence on occasion for the better part of three years and never done that.

I put her in her pen and she discovered that if she leaped at the side she could move it across the floor; she could move it across the garden; she could climb it and overset it and have it come apart and then she could attack Puma and mean it. Puma seemed for ever in flight; puppy for ever in pursuit, trying to boss Big Dogs.

Her haul by then, as well as the gloves, was three leads, bitten right through, and two collars, eaten off Puma's neck as they lay side by side in the evening. She managed to eat two more woollen gloves, stolen from the hall drawer, opening it by tugging on the handle, which I didn't believe till I caught her doing it. She ate a hat. She cost a fortune – I could hardly bombard the insurance people. They'd probably double our premium.

She jumped on to my desk and gnawed three rubbers, one of which she hid so thoroughly it was a month before I found it, jammed under a box in the study.

She discovered how to open a door that had successfully kept the other two inside the room ever since we moved. I didn't know she had and was busy at the time. I had put her in her pen. I heard a yell. She had gone up the stairs, which are open plan, and had fallen and was wedged in the bannisters, held by the middle, struggling madly.

She was then eight months old.

I called, 'Chita, stay', and it worked. She relaxed, and I lifted her out and was rewarded for the first time by a puppy that climbed into my arms and leaned her head on my shoulder for a cuddle; a position she liked so much that it became a habit so long as Big Dogs weren't there. Had her temperament been really impossible, she would have bitten me as she struggled; but she hadn't. It gave me hope for the future. Just puppy madness and an extra mad puppy. We *would* make progress.

By now Kenneth was tolerating her, though she did her best to win him over – those tiny drops of water still defeated her.

She now, if free, raced round the field at top speed, a speed that outdistanced Puma; she was growing but not very much and still appeared very tiny. Everything grew at a different rate and she was out of proportion. Her eyes still had that old-fashioned look and also, when she lost her temper, which she did if anything or anyone refused to do what she wanted (including cats and Big Dogs), her eyes changed and took on a very wild look that worried me. I thought I had imagined it until other people commented. Later, I saw the same look in her nephew. It worried his owner too.

Racing round the field had hazards. She went so fast she collided with the fence and jammed her head between two bars. She yelled at the top of her voice and the older dogs rushed to see what was wrong, and Puma came flying to me, telling me to hurry up, puppy was in trouble again. No matter how much she tormented them, neither of them bore her any ill will, and when she condescended to play properly and nicely, they played enthusiastically with her.

I managed to push the posts apart and release her. The noise stopped and off she went, this time on the lead, soberly down the field.

Soberly? She saw a bird and lunged; she had lunged down the steps the other day and I'd fallen, almost breaking my neck. If I didn't get her under control soon she *would* break my neck, or my leg, as she was most amazingly strong.

Once more I asked for help from a police-dog handler and he suggested my coming over with her. She still raved at other dogs, so we spent an hour walking her between two police dogs, till the raving stopped and she settled down. He confirmed my opinion that it was fear that made her do it. She was saying "Go away, I hate you. I'll kill you before you kill me."

Would I like to try a track with her?

What a silly question!

Chita adored tracking and off she went at top speed, found her yellow plastic bunny, and was given it to play with.

"Let her off."

"She won't come back."

"Of course she will."

I knew better, but I let her off and she had great fun, racing around, carrying her yellow bunny, throwing it in the air and playing with it. Call her, and away she went at top speed, demented little object, refusing every blandishment.

We called her and we called her; we threw things for her; coaxed her, walked away from her, whistled to her. Come? Not she. I had been teaching her for weeks to come. She would come at home, but here, with freedom to run, in the middle of a deserted military barracks that we had all to ourselves, no way.

"OK, we'll try something else."

So off went one of us to lie almost full length by the wall, and my instructor and I lay down side by side flat on our backs and looked at a grey wintry sky, which was as prepossessing as the sea in December. It felt remarkably silly, and I was glad there was no one about.

People lying down.

How very odd.

What are they doing?

She came close and sniffed us, and I was told not to move. I was glad I was wearing rainproof clothing. Even through trousers and anorak, the ground felt very cold.

She came up to me, and curled against me. "Must be resting time for me too." Very gently, I snapped on the lead. A good three quarters of an hour had been wasted, and it meant that I needed to spend far more time on getting her to come. A long line daily: "Chita, come," over and over and over and over. And, being Chita, she always obeyed on the line and never off it.

At home she decided she was a working dog and a working dog works. It works all day and it apparently works all night. Work to Chita meant jumping; meant running, meant being with me constantly, asking to be walked, to be taken out to jump, over the big-scale jump which was now all of two feet high; over the long jump, which was all of two feet long, and over the hurdle, also at two feet. Flattening the molehills, "Chita, dig." She dug. The moles were extremely active, and so was Chita. She flattened them thoroughly.

If anything was in her way when she was running free she jumped it. She also jumped Puma and Janus instead of going round them; she jumped the four-foot wall, though she wasn't supposed to. She jumped anything and everything she could, including a friend's husband sitting at table, when we went visiting. He wasn't pleased.

She was long-lined for about ten minutes twice a day. "Chita, come," and Chita did. Off lead, "Chita, come," and Chita didn't.

By now, the little room at Brynsiencyn was too small for all the dogs and, talking it over one day, someone suggested we asked the Town Clerk if we could have a room in the Community Centre, where the vet has a surgery and many people hold meetings; some of them prayer meetings, some of them other community projects. It proved possible to get the room on Tuesday evening. No other evening was free so we agreed to change our day, otherwise we would have to give up as far too many dogs were coming for our tiny little hall.

I took Chita in whenever I wasn't teaching, which was rare, as it took two of us all our time to keep things going but, when Vera took the class, then I was able to try my little demon.

And demon she was. I wondered what people made of her, as there was I teaching them and my own dog behaved like an idiot, totally untrained to all appearances. When I felt really desperate, I took Janus in and was delighted at the Christmas competition when I competed with Chita, but not Janus. Janus did the initial round to show what ought to be done; and there was a spontaneous burst of applause as he behaved perfectly, delighted to be the centre of attention once more, as pup took up far too much of my time and still was anything but civilised and biddable.

Chita came third out of about twenty. She would have been first, but she decided when on downstay to snarl at the dog beside her and I had to put my foot on her lead and lose points, or she would have been up and attacking. I was exhausted trying to train her and felt life must be easier in some way, but how, I didn't know. I never dared relax when I had her out with me.

I couldn't praise her, as if praised she promptly tried to leap on to my shoulder and lick my face!

"I am clever, aren't I clever, you did say I was clever? Great".

She was more like a kangaroo than a dog, and greeted all the family with that enormous leap, straight up in the air on her hind legs. It wasn't fierce, but some people thought it was and it had to be stopped too, but how? Her reactions are ten times as fast as mine. A knee in her chest was funny. She didn't care.

When I got really desperate, I sat down and ticked off the things she *did* do right. She had learned that food only came when she was sitting still and *quiet*, as if she made a noise I simply took the older dogs and their food into another room and came back and stood quite still in front of her till it dawned on her she had to shut up.

I did the same thing when she yelled to get out of the car. Out came Big Dogs and off I went, to return when she was silent again. I was tired of losing my voice trying to out-yell her. It also dawned, but slowly, as she appeared at times to be unbelievably stupid.

She knew 'bed' and went there when told. She lay still in the evening while we watched TV, if you can consider lying like a coiled-up spring ready to explode lying still. At least she didn't bumble round like a lunatic, which is something I can't stand in a dog. If they are in the house they behave, all of them, as three dogs their size crashing round is far from sensible and things get damaged.

She occasionally walked properly on the lead but I had to abandon all idea of taking the three dogs out together as she snapped at Puma if she walked by her, snapped at Janus if she walked by him and, if she walked on her own, she lunged constantly, knowing I couldn't check her when the other two were there. The kind of check she needed was something that I couldn't get nearly enough power into; she needed a tough uncompromising man to deal with her. Had she been owned by an enormous deep-voiced very stern man, she'd probably have been no problem. Our neighbour's collie needs all his strength – and still doesn't always behave! And his master farms for his living.

I was changing all my ideas about the way you train a dog. I had never had a dog before that was a real hard case. Janus by comparison had been child's play to train. Puma was so easy it was unbelievable; and now my older dogs gave me more pleasure than ever before. They were good, and they were quiet, they came when called, did as told, walked on the lead sensibly, and had settled down into very rewarding animals. They'd never won Obedience competitions but who cares – there's more to life than that. I could enjoy my walks with them, and relax.

It had taken time and patience, but it had never taken the amount of time and patience that this one needed. I no longer thought of training for competition – neither Obedience nor Working Trials. I was training for CONTROL. The basics are the same.

Train her when I got up. 'Stay, Chita, stay.' Stay? I had to be joking. Sitstays meant to move backwards fast on her tail, away from me, even on the lead. I put her back again and again and again. I needed help, as no one, even those teaching in dog clubs, knew what to do with her, and the only advice I got was the inevitable, "Put her down."

If I could train her . . .

One friend said, "One thing, she's no end of a challenge; if you can train her she might be something really first class."

I looked at her doing a downstay in the club. On lead, perfect; the second the lead came off, she crept on her tummy towards me. Snap on the lead and I got an angel; take it off, and she moved and moved again. Put her back and start again.

She knew every movement I made. She knew when I could check her and when the lead was off; she knew she was free to do as she chose.

Other dogs in the club improved. Chita appeared to and I could now walk her at heel and have her look good. She wasn't good, but she was better; in the hall, fine. Out of the hall, I had a maniac, fighting the lead like a salmon on a line. Let her off, and she went for other dogs and chased anything that moved. She never went off lead anywhere now.

Check her and praise her; check her and praise her. Teach her to jump. No problem there; I did get results and she enjoyed it, doing what she wanted to do. Teach her to come. Fine on the lead, perfect on the lead, knowing she was under my control. Off lead, I had to be joking.

I took her visiting, to Janet, who had two bearded collies, a border collie and a very old Basenji; Chita wasn't sure about the border collie, who wasn't sure about her, but they behaved – even Chita. We spent several weekends together, as Janet also teaches in dog club and gave me some useful ideas on training my fireball of energy.

We stayed with Gina, who had several border collies and two German Shepherds, one of them a distant relative of Chita's. Like Chita, in her early days she had snapped; but she had been cured and was now a lovely easy bitch, giving me hope. I found that one particular dog in her ancestry was likely to produce snapping in his descendants. Gina took me to Newbury Dog Club, and also to supper with John Simpson, who had just won Crufts with his lovely German Shepherd, Courage. Sadly, Courage died soon after. I was very glad I'd been lucky enough to meet him. He was a beautiful, kind dog.

We stayed with my publisher, who had two spaniels, and a number of times with Joy, who had two Shelties; the year before, with Honor, who had three dogs; and with John Cree, who had two German Shepherds. Chita was afraid of Jeza, but Jeza just flapped a big paw when Chita flipped, and said, 'Come off it, silly pup,' very kindly, and Chita did.

We went training with around twenty dogs, at a Scottish training club that practised for Working Trials.

We visited Chita's father; a lovely furry friendly dog, with no sign of any of the faults that bugged me with Chita. Some of his other daughters were as small as she was. His owner, who is a Championship Judge as well as a very famous breeder, measured Chita. She was 23″ – right in the middle of the standard size for bitches. She is short in body which gives an illusion of small size.

We visited our own family. Andrew's Scruffy happily accepted Chita as well as the other two dogs; she knew them already. Chita accepted her. We could never mix Wolf, our other son's Labrador, and Janus, so didn't attempt to let Wolf meet Chita.

When we weren't visiting, I took Chita tracking. Anywhere on her own she was good; anywhere other dogs were liable to appear she was an absolute nuisance; she never did bite the other dog, but she looked so evil, snarling, her lips back and that odd light in her eye, the really wild look that worried me and bothered other people.

In spite of this, I realised she was far from typical; and I hope I will never be without a German Shepherd; Puma fortunately restored the balance, as by now she was all pleasure to own, and when Chita had exhausted me beyond measure, I would put her in her crate in the car and play with the two older dogs, who revelled in being 'only' dogs again. Bring Chita out, and she still immediately went for Puma, bullying her mercilessly, until Puma came to me, or raced to the car, asking to be put in, to enjoy peace and quiet, or stood by the house door, begging me to let her go in again. Puma would never come out of the house if Chita were free on the field.

It wasn't easy to find time to write, as the pup took so much time. She did behave, lying down quietly, but she seemed to have inherited a leaky tank that wasn't totally under her control, and she still puddled in excitement, or in fear, and had to be taken out more often than the older dogs. Also, she still drank a good deal more than the other two. I had tests done on her but she was absolutely normal.

I have Chita's niece in the dog club now. She invariably makes a puddle when she greets me! So it's obviously in the breeding.

Puma never behaved like that, even as a baby.

The dog club was building up, making a new interest and it's fascinating to notice friendships beginning; people greet one another, sit together, go off together afterwards, meet inbetween whiles. Many have dogs with minor problems. Some come for a night out and a friendly atmosphere, and now we are getting into our swing we are planning to do more. Some of us are beginning to track together.

We had a road safety test which was very successful, a sponsored 'downstay' which raised over a hundred and fifty pounds for the Guide Dog we want to provide for someone who is blind. We were asked to put on three demonstrations. The starting of the club helped me with

Chita in that it gave me something else to think about besides her problems, and it also meant I could bring her in among understanding people; they were all rather appalled when she flew out at their dogs, but I had her very well leashed and was ready for it, and slowly she learned she must accept other dogs. She was never in a position to harm any dog, and after a few fraught minutes she settled and behaved.

I met dog club members at other times, and once Chita knew a dog all was well. Meet a new dog and the demon in her took over, and I began to wonder if she was schizophrenic; an angel one minute, a devil the next. It was a disturbing thought in a dog. She wasn't, of course. She had merely learned through a very unpleasant experience that other dogs could be dangerous.

I enrolled on Charlie Wyant's course, wanting help from anyone who would give me clues to my puppy. Charlie is one of the oldest professionals in the Obedience field; he has trained four champions and helped train many more; his course was at his home near Canterbury.

I went down in May and stayed at The Woodpecker in Womenswold, not far from the Dover Road. I hadn't been back to Kent for years and I went back in blossom time, when the trees were ablaze with flowers, when the whole country looked its best, when the sun shone and the voices around me were my childhood voices.

It was all too brief. I was wildly and violently homesick for the South and the folk in Kent and a way of life that seemed quite different, though I don't suppose it is.

I learned a great deal from Charlie, but I didn't learn what made Chita tick; he liked her, as she was enthusiastic and eager and, of course, being a first-class handler, he could take her and she obeyed him. And being a large man used to dogs, she did not try to challenge him, as she knows very well who can outwit her and who can't; and men are far more powerful than women, physically.

Everyone there had dogs; some had four or five; there must have been about forty people and about eighty dogs in all. Charlie thought it would be a good idea to let Chita run free with other dogs on the field. I wasn't so sure, but he knew more than I. All went very happily, till one day a big grey sable German Shepherd bitch chased Chita round the field. Chita had never been chased before; she had been bitten, which didn't help at all; she was still liable to flip when dogs came near. This time she had no chance; the bitch raced at her snarling and Chita took off, the bitch in close pursuit. "She does that," said the owner, who was in grave danger of being assaulted by me, as a bitch known to be like that should not have been allowed off lead near other dogs.

There was no way to stop or catch them. I ran, as Chita made straight for the main road, a busy, twisting road, a speed track, traffic roaring along it all day, as it is very near to Dover. Charlie had a gem of a kennel help who was used to pups and who reacted fast. As the pup came racing along, she blocked her and scooped her up, safely, holding the terrified morsel close, talking to her softly and I was able to take her.

Re-assure her?

Not Chita.

She hadn't been bitten this time but she had been well and truly terrified, and all my work with her was undone. Up to that day she had behaved herself; now she went for every single dog she saw, including Janus and Puma. She snarled at them in the car. I took her and walked her on her own, but it was night time before she was safe with the two of them. She slept in my room, so she was under my eyes all night. I slept lightly, waking every time she moved.

Next day as we came out of the car, Chita attacked Puma again.

I went to find Charlie, who suggested I tie Chita by the door so that every single dog that came had to pass her; ignore her, and let her fly out; she couldn't keep it up all day. She didn't keep it up all day and by the end of the week we had just about returned to where we were before; she wasn't too bad as long as she didn't see a collie or a German Shepherd.

The Obedience world is made up, almost entirely, of both.

There was nothing to do but make a list of everyone I knew with both and take Chita there to meet them, over and over again.

I remembered an odd little rhyme someone had once told me:

'The marines when they got to heaven,
Found St Peter, who said, "Oh well,
Come right in and sit down, boys,
You've served your time in hell."'

I seemed to be timeserving in a dog owner's hell; I began to wonder what I had done in past lives to deserve Chita. She was adorable when she was good but she was such a fiend when other dogs were around. My first evening back at the dog club confirmed all my fears. We were right back at the beginning.

"Joyce's new dog is an utter swine." I suspect 'swine' was a substitute for a much more forceful word.

Ian's words came back, time and time again. He hadn't much help for me; there wasn't time; though when I went over, all the dog handlers around helped by bringing out their dogs; their dogs tolerated Chita nobly. Silly baby.

Why was she like that? Was it just fear of other dogs? She did have very good cause.

Always the old dog-club tenet recurs; it is the handler, not the dog. So what am I doing wrong? Is it me? I was pretty certain most people were sure it was me; but, I kept reminding myself, most people hadn't had a dog like Chita; most people didn't have her breed. And then I met the local RSPCA inspector, who said that many of her breed locally get put down as totally uncontrollable.

That wasn't funny at all.

At home to make matters, which were bad enough, even worse, Casey, my male Siamese cat, was turning vicious and behaving very oddly. Though neutered, every time we had visitors he sprayed their clothes; he sprayed my grandson's pram; and he bit my accountant so badly he had to have hospital treatment.

I didn't know if he was jealous of Chita; maybe he had a brain tumour. He was also bullying his sister mercilessly so that two or three times a day the air was loud with their fighting, and Siamese cats fighting make as much noise as Chita in one of her paddies. The only thing that outdid them was next door's litter of pigs at feeding time. I couldn't believe anything could make more noise than Chita and Casey, but those little pigs screamed the heavens down.

I was beginning to feel extremely miserable and very fed up. Chita continued to rave at other dogs and Casey continued to become more and more unpleasant to live with.

Chita was now quiet and easy so long as I was driving, so I took to visiting people at a considerable distance and staying with them for distant shows; two long days in the car meant two long days during which I didn't have to discipline her. She needed far more voice and far more strength than the other two, and now she was maturing she was becoming even more dominant.

I had had Chita less than a year. One thing that I had learned from Charlie did help. He used a cotton square, about twelve inches by twelve inches with a knot in the middle, to attract his pup's attention as he walked beside it and make it look up. If only Chita would do this, then she might stay at heel and not lunge out. At home, she loved it; it was great fun, and so was racing after the rag and bringing it back; and so was finding it hidden up the field.

I still needed more help than I was getting, but where on earth could I go for it?

It had to be somewhere near; I badly needed someone to help me with my dog. I was helping others with theirs and no one taught me, or watched me work, knew if she were walking wide or turning right, or sitting correctly. Not that it mattered, I suppose, since shows were a misery with her and people steered clear. I couldn't talk to *anyone* if I were holding Chita. I needed all my attention on her. If I relaxed, she promptly lunged and yelled at passing dogs.

I had started a puppy class at the vet's suggestion. My first pupils were four little Scotties, all from the same litter who came together, and were the greatest fun. Each one different, each one endearing, and it was heaven to have easy pups, pups I could relax with, watch with amusement, and pups that later for a little while came to dog club with their owners. Their mother came too, and I watched a little Scottie train go round the room, mum and four babies, all in line, looking delightful.

Three dropped out, but Tammie still comes with her young owner and is one of my successes. It is so much better to start classes with nice little puppies as soon as inoculations are completed, as although you can't do formal training then, you can get a puppy used to people, noises, places, and other dogs; and you don't, with normal puppies, get shyness developing at six months. That is the worst time of all, to start class as the dog is beginning to mature and is rather mixed up and suddenly faced with a whole lot of daunting new situations. If he has come from the time he is first able to go out, it isn't new; it is familiar, and formal training starts under better conditions. Unfortunately, pups are a bit of a nuisance and many clubs won't take them, thereby defeating everything in dog training. Older dogs need *re*-training – not just training.

Charlie Wyant and many others like him start teaching the puppy at five weeks old, even before, as what happens in its first eight weeks may affect it later. If not handled, it will be shy; if alarmed by other dogs, it may become fierce; if brought into the house, it will never be house shy and, given only pleasant experiences, will take household noises in its stride. This had been done, so far as I know, with Chita, so that in that respect I never had any bother at all. She knew all about machinery and radios and TV.

The Scotties were joined by two Airedales. Then came several German Shepherds and a spaniel, and a couple of Poodles; and I found I was busy again, which was wonderful. I was writing hard, but Chita had a habit of interfering with that, as she wasn't always quiet when I was writing. Or she needed to go out fast; and also she needed to be kept far more occupied than any dog I had ever known, as she had to *work*. So life had to be geared to make Chita *think* she was working. I got the manual of police-dog training; I began to re-read my American training books as they do train dogs; we tend to tickle the problem, and problem dogs which can be kept sane by training may go wild because no one recognises their need or utilises it.

Few men take it kindly when they are out of work; few women like having nothing at all to do, ever; yet many dogs that need to be worked lie by the fire, have a brief walk and that is their lot. Every dog in this country, even the Poodle, came originally from working stocks. A properly taught Poodle is extremely intelligent; all the sheepdogs did once herd sheep, even if some are only show dogs now; all the gundogs did work in the field, even if some are now half the size they used to be and barely capable of staggering round the ring, posing for the cameras.

When I was in Scotland, I took Chita to a homeopathic doctor recommended to me, who suggested she might have worms that hadn't been identified. She proved to have a hookworm, which is rare except where there are sheep and pigs; we have both around us. Next door's pig sometimes grazes our bottom field, so now I never let the dogs through there. It can also come from kennels. The problem has never recurred.

We dosed her. The dogs are dosed regularly and all should be, but I had Janus tested (he is always worm free) as with his odd digestion the pills could upset him. Once Chita had been wormed, I decided to have the bitches tested too in case Puma had picked up hookworm. The tests are done through the vet. All the dogs were worm free, and have been ever since; I know, as I get the tests repeated twice a year. It saves a lot of worry.

If there are children in the family it is well worth the money (the price of two gallons of petrol at the 1979 rate) to make quite sure there is absolutely no parasite that could harm them. A great deal is said in the press about the dangers of dog infection, but this can only happen if the family is careless about hygiene and doesn't bother to see that the dog is properly kept. Clean dogs never cause trouble. One quick spray gets rid of fleas, so I never understand people who say you can't help dogs catching them; for less than £1, you can immediately get rid of them. I spray the dogs once a fortnight, just in case, as the spray stays in the fur and lasts for that long, killing anything the dog may pick up. Dead birds and hedgehogs harbour fleas.

Spraying is part of their grooming; none of my dogs object to it.

I also learned that with Chita, nothing could be done in a hurry; she excited too fast. If I rushed, she rushed with me, screaming and leaping, to go wherever I was going, be it to the phone or the door. So I slowed down; not easy as it isn't natural. Slowly to the door, pup beside me. "It's OK, no hurry, calm down, little girl. Easy-easy."

Slowly to the phone. I always allowed at least half an hour to get her ready to go out; trying never to be rushed or she was impossible; and so were passengers likely to hold me up, as when Chita got excited she got above herself and turned on the other dogs, snarling and snapping, which Janus wouldn't tolerate if he was feeling off colour. Normally he was remarkably patient with her, and had a way of looking at me, a comical expression on his face. "These young fry. We're above all that, aren't we?"

The one place he couldn't stand her noise was in the car. Neither could I, so we were in total accord over that.

I went on going to shows for I knew I must get Chita socialised somehow. I entered Janus. I did enter Chita once or twice, but it was hopeless to try and work a bitch that either rushed at other dogs yelling at them, or shied behind me, scared out of its mind.

All the same, she did have an interesting nature, when she relaxed. She learned what she wanted to learn fast; no way would she learn if she didn't want to. She enjoyed heelwork, but I had to walk slowly or she leaped at me and bit my hand. As I had arthritis in my hands and they were extremely painful, this was intolerable. If I walked slowly, she kept beside me. I got told off by judges who interpret the Kennel Club's rule of "Dog must work in a happy natural manner", as being a need to march them round at top speed with the dog at top speed beside you. If you slow down you are told you are 'pacing your dog'. I wasn't pacing Chita, she was pacing me. And since in the top classes you do slow, fast, and normal pace with the dog keeping in step, I have never worked out why, when I walk more slowly than some, I should slow down a dog that would have me racing at the top of both our speeds, biting at my hands; I should be told to speed it up! Walk fast with Chita, and she behaved impossibly, leaping at my hands, zany and inaccurate. My slower pace was approved by John Holmes who, when he came to talk to our dog club and saw her, suggested I never walked her fast.

Slower pacing calmed her considerably. A fast pace excited her.

I went to the German Shepherd League rally, which was great fun. There was an assault course of jumps and Chita adored it; she had to scale, and since scaling at home meant coming back, though she wasn't supposed to, she did go back, and I had to put her over again, afraid she would continue to yo-yo over the six-foot scale for the rest of the day. She didn't. Being a grandmother doesn't help my speed; I took one and three-quarter minutes to complete the course, against nineteen seconds for the winner, who was about nineteen! However, she did every jump except the water jump, which she paddled through, enjoying that too; and she repeated the round, bettering our speed by a quarter of a second! The course was uphill, which didn't help me. At one point I had to dive through a suspended motor tyre, something I hadn't done for a good many years, not since the obstacle race in my schooldays. Chita watched me astounded. She didn't have to come too but come she did, eager not to be left out.

John Cree was there, with another friend, [illegible] both with their dogs to put on a Working Trial demonstration, which I watched. John had organised another event; a novice round to be done with the handler blindfold. In the novice round the dog has to walk close by the handler on lead; right turns, left turns and about turns, and sit at the halts, of which there are several. The same off lead. Then it has to be called to sit in front of the handler, and finish by going behind her, tightly, and sitting straight at her left side; and then retrieve a dumb-bell, to finish in the same way.

It isn't easy with full sight. Blindfold it is nearly impossible, and our only comfort was that most people messed it. I didn't dare try Chita so I tried Puma, who apparently took one look at me standing there with a scarf over my eyes and went on strike, sitting watching me cavort round the ring on my own till the recall, which she did do. I don't know what she did with the dumb-bell. I shall never forget the look on her face when I took the scarf off. If ever a dog could have said "People are quite mad," she would have said it then.

I would have liked to have tried with Janus, but his breed is outlawed at German Shepherd shows so he had to be walked discreetly, a golden-coloured freak among all the Alsatians. "What's that? Funny looking Alsatian," people joked. It was nice to re-meet people I had known for a long time, and after that competition I put the older dogs back in the car and took Chita, who seemed to have relaxed after the assault course.

Or so I thought.

I met someone with four of Puma's great-granddaughters; they might have been quads, they were so alike. Very like Puma at that age (five months), with gentle faces, lovely shapes, and that same beautiful head with wonderful wise eyes and a kind expression. I looked at them; perfectly behaved, alert and interested, watching everything that went on. I looked down at my little dark horror. If only she would behave, just this once, just for the whole day; so far she hadn't been too bad.

I went to talk to Bert, whose wife breeds German Shepherds. Bert bred horses; he had been retired a long time, but if you wanted good honest down-to-earth advice on dogs, he was the man for it. Talking to him, joking, I relaxed, which was unwise as someone passed us close and Chita flashed out, roaring.

"Go away, beastly dog. I hate dogs."

"Bloody hell, Joyce," Bert said. "Give me that thing. She needs teaching she can't go on behaving like that. I could cure her in a week if I had her; you'll have to let me. She can't go on behaving like that."

I watched him. He has immense strength and I don't. As Chita lunged, Bert snatched at the lead and she came flying back to him, astounded beyond measure. So astounded, she stood there, meekly, unable to make up her mind what had happened. It was all very well for Bert; he was ten times as strong as I was. Few men realise women just don't have the muscular power in their bodies that the male sex has. I am all for equality, but no one is going to convince me I can work like a docker or a navvy because I know I can't. A lot of men can't either, so I suppose it isn't all that one-sided.

"Do that every time she flies out, and stop her doing it," Bert said.

I tried, but Chita was fast and Chita was strong and my hands weren't strong enough for her.

I had a number of choices left.

I could give up and put her down. Maybe I ought to. But I had another major problem as Casey had bitten a friend of mine very badly and I knew that he would do it again; I knew that the problem wasn't getting easier, as he was also vicious with Chia, his sister, who led a hunted life, mostly in the wardrobe where she could hide from him.

Casey was going to have to go; I tried everything I could and so did the vet, but the day was coming. I couldn't put two animals down. I had to get Chita right.

Bert suggested a much less high protein diet; to cut down her oats, as one did a very lively horse or pony. Give them too much oats and horses are impossible to train. Instead of letting her run off her energy as other people had suggested, lots of long calming downstays; downstay for ever if she would. As soon as she got excited, tell her 'Down'. If I let her run free, she ended up like a little overwound toy, more and more excited, yelling and snapping at the other dogs, leaping in and snapping at me, not viciously but in an excess of energy she simply couldn't control.

I wished I had never seen the puppy. I wished I had bought one of the pups I met so often, the same breed, but so different. They came to my dog club and I could take them and they were total pleasure. They were alert and interested and I had to keep Chita away from them in case she went for them and upset them.

She was a confounded nuisance, to put it mildly.

Chapter Seven

It wasn't a good summer; the weather was wretched and Kenneth's boating holidays were a disaster as they were constantly cold and wet. He went to Scotland with friends. They endured gales and rain, and were perpetually chilly. I went down to my mother, just before the League rally, and stayed a fortnight; part of it with her, part of it in a caravan loaned to me by friends, as I felt my two aunts, who usually had us to stay, could not cope that summer. One of them had had a slight stroke and life wasn't easy for them. I could visit them, but three dogs and two rather elderly ladies seemed to me unwise.

My mother's Westie wasn't too happy about Chita; I wasn't too happy about Chita. Lucky didn't want this intruder in her home, though Janus and Puma had been several times before. She wasn't too worried about them. I was extremely worried about my pup.

Lucky ran at her barking. "Go away. This is my house."

To my surprise, Chita didn't retaliate, then or at any other time. Either she recognised this wasn't her territory, or that Lucky was afraid of her and, if that was so, then she would be benevolent. It was the first sign I had seen of any sense on her part. I began to hope against hope that it was the beginning of a new phase and that she was maturing.

The visit went off well. We went to Worthing. The night before the show I went with my friends Anne and Pat to the chairman's house to get the last-minute details right, and Ron suggested I bring Chita in. She behaved like a total lunatic; she wouldn't settle, she wouldn't obey me, she wouldn't even obey him when he used all his voice on her. Ron breeds Boxers, which aren't the easiest of breeds, and has had a lot of experience. He is also an all rounder Breed judge.

His views of her were much the same as Ian's: "She's a little horror".

He found her small and steep-shouldered breedwise, which I already knew; and not at all good temperament wise. He didn't say so, but I could see he felt I would never do a thing with her. I was banging my head against a brick wall. She needed the sort of voice he used on villains – or she just ignored him. He wrote a report on her for the German Shepherd Improvement Society, in which he said that she would not, at any time, respond to a normal voice, but needed a very harsh tone indeed before she would obey any command.

Matters didn't improve next day at the Show, when she went for several dogs. I worked Janus, but not very well, as Chita seemed to dominate my thinking. When I got home I would have to do something about Casey, whom I shouldn't keep either.

We went back to Anne and Pat's home, where Anne's new Samoyed puppy was a ball of gorgeous white fluff; and Pat's old boy Butch, who they call Grandfather, cast a slightly wary eye over Chita and retired to his bed. Chita found Sailor's bones and made off with them. We removed all bones. I didn't think Anne was too happy about Chita; I kept a very firm eye on my little bitch. Janus and Puma went out to play in the garden but she didn't. Pat did comfort me, as Butch had been a quite impossibly tempered dog. Now he was as amiable as any, and no one believed the stories of his younger days, when he was the terror of the neighbourhood, though not with quite the same oddities as Chita. By now, talking with Ron and Anne and Pat who all taught in dog club and had done for a good many years, I realised *she* was odd, and it wasn't me at all. If it had been, the other two dogs would have been just as bad with all other dogs.

This was reassuring in one way. Not in another, as it might be something I could never cure.

I stayed, en route, with another dog friend and her three dogs; Chita behaved once she had got over the initial introduction. Voicing my fears, I was told once more that if it were my fault, Janus and Puma would also be vicious, so I shouldn't worry so much. She was gorgeous with people, so I had only to cure her going for other dogs.

Ha, ha, seemed to be the only reply to that, but I came home more determined than ever to get someone to help me. I went back to Ian and the dog handlers, and over to my other police-dog handler friend; I tried checking her as Bert had done but hadn't enough power to do so.

My hands were still swollen and painful.

Then I saw an advertisement in *Dog Training Weekly* for a weekend handlers' course. I knew of Edith who was running it, as I had been on a course at Llanelli some years before, run by John Seal, whose Obedience champion collie, Bett, had been very well known all over the country. Edith was going to share my chalet, but she also ran a café at the time and in the end was too busy to come. As a result, I had never met her.

I wasn't even sure where the place was, but found, rather to my surprise, it was only forty miles away. Easy enough to get there. I would try it.

The form came and I filled it in. One section was for problems with dogs. I wrote down my problems with Chita and wondered what they would make of them – or me, for that matter.

It is never easy meeting a whole lot of new people. I went over feeling exhausted and not very well. My hands were sore and swollen; it was November and very cold; we had flurries of snow. There were all kinds of people there, some with much better dogs than Janus, workwise, some with worse. No one had a dog like Chita. I not only had to give her a good deal of exercise but, owing to her uncontrollable bladder, had to go to bed very late and get up very early, as she wailed to go out and *had* to go out. I was so tired I was going to have problems in reacting fast with her; in that sort of company I was pretty sure everyone would say 'It's the handler, not the dog.'

The first night was easy. I was sleeping in the hotel, where I had a little room opposite the kitchen and near the back door. It had a shower, and I could bring the dogs in.

It was bitterly cold, as the electricians were wiring that wing and the power was off, but I was given a Calor gas stove and a hot-water bottle and that made it much more pleasant. The first night all the handlers met and talked; there was a lecture on dog handling, and Edith and Bob introduced themselves. It was our first meeting; I often wondered what they said about me afterwards as I must have presented a picture of someone with a dog I couldn't control, as I had once before with Janus, treating it quite wrongly. I now know what they did say!

I need not have worried about Edith anyway, as she breeds German Shepherds and it was quickly apparent, once she started to talk, that she knew a great deal more than most about the breed, approaching it in the same way as Puma's breeder. Later she was able to tell me about dogs in the past; about faults in the past.

I came out in the morning well wrapped up, as it was starting to snow. There was snow on the hills. I brought Chita out. Bob was just coming out of the kennels and Edith was sorting out the two classes. Chita lunged lunatically, screaming, at the end of her lead, as someone came past with a young German Shepherd.

Bob took my hateful bitch off me and gave her a lesson similar to that Bert had given her, but harder. There was a minute or two of confrontation. Chita didn't like discipline.

He handed her back, saying nothing, but giving me an odd look. He had been an Army instructor and he is a no nonsense person. He'd tell you straight and tell you the truth; he never minced words or wrapped up hard facts.

It was only a few weeks since Casey had been put down. I felt mean, as he was a healthy cat, but he had had a field day; he had sprayed my car and Kenneth's Land Rover, a sack of potatoes, the bread, which was on the draining board, had had a really nasty fight with his sister, Chia, and scratched Liz's little son, attacking him for no reason at all as he sat on the floor. Liz worked for me and had been very patient with Casey. I had taken him, while I was still angry, straight into his cage, and over to the vet, who agreed the time had come. He had injured three people, badly, and he appeared to be not quite sane. All the same Casey in his more reasonable moments had been a sweet cat; he had adored me, even to the last, purring because he was my cat; he ought maybe to have been an only animal; but there was nothing I could do about that. He had had several chances. But I minded very much.

So when Bob that night took me aside and said, "Joyce, that dog of yours is a real Jekyll and Hyde character, the way she is today. There's only one answer, a one-way trip to the vet for her," I knew I couldn't face it. Also, I had put over a year's work into her. I had paid a good price for her. I had spent time and trouble on her, as well as bearing the cost of her keep and vet bills, and I didn't want to lose on my investment in her. If I could get her under control it would be a real victory, as I now knew I did have something very out of the ordinary. I wished I knew which ancestors had caused her major problems, as I knew pups which had one or other of Chita's ancestors in their pedigree and none of them was like her. None of the pups I knew had *all* her ancestors though, and that could well have been the trouble. I found out later it was, but it doesn't happen with *every* pup bred the same way, only with some of them.

I went to talk to Edith, feeling she might have more understanding of a tom-fool female than Bob. She had, but she was dubious, and asked if I realised what would be involved; not just the intensive training, which Chita needed desperately to get her under my total control, but to establish for always that *I* was boss and no way could she defy me as she was doing. Also it was not just a case of training a dog, but of re-educating a dog that had a major personality problem; one that would get much worse if she had her own way. And of training *me* to a standard I had never dreamed about – capable of re-training major problem dogs.

I had another reason for wanting to get on top of Chita, as I now had two more similar to her at my puppy class. They had been bred from a different bitch, but Chita's brother was their father. One was a dog belonging to a woman who had had two German Shepherds before him and who was doing her best to cope with a puppy such as she had never seen before. The other was a woman who had never had a dog in her life, and not only didn't know how to train a dog, but didn't realise that her dog wasn't like other dogs she had met and needed far more firmness than she was giving it. They were twelve weeks old when they started. By six months, in spite of very hard work, we had progressed backwards. Both were unruly and totally wild. If I could get Chita under control, maybe I could help them.

I told Edith about them and told her about the dog club. I told her I had no one to discuss dogs with and discovered to my relief and pleasure that she was determined to up-grade the standard of training in the clubs wherever she could. Also, she was planning later in the year a course to help dog-club instructors become more knowledgeable; to take in the real problem dog as opposed to the dog whose owner thinks he has problems, most of which are caused by wrong handling in the first place. Unfortunately, even with good intentions, the clubs cannot cope with very unruly dogs unless the owners co-operate fully. The owner *must* do all the work. Dog clubs teach the owners. The owners teach the dogs, at home during the week . . .

When Edith heard about the club she agreed to help me; it was going to take time; not a week or two but maybe more than a year. If I were prepared to do as she instructed, to do it to the best of my ability and to learn far more than I already knew, I might be successful. It was extremely good of her and I appreciated it enormously, as she was very busy with boarding dogs and training them professionally.

Talking with her, I realised that at last I had found someone with the type of knowledge I needed; not just knowledge of dogs, but of how to train dogs of all types for all types of work. She had to plan the exercises to steady the dog and get it under control with distractions; she took in problem dogs and re-educated them. I didn't want to hand over Chita as *I* needed the experience. If it did come through Chita's breeding, there were going to be one or two in many litters like her from kennels all over the country; and it was very probable they would be sold to people who had even less experience than I, and less will to change themselves. You can't change the dog; you can only train it to control it. Hand it over to someone who does *not* control it, and the dog reverts to its horrible habits.

Edith showed me what to do and how to do it, but I still hadn't the strength in my hands. I saw her looking at them. They were a mess, the knuckles swollen and shiny and very painful. I could keep them from looking too bad by using face cream to hide the really odd appearance that comes with arthritis. I didn't want medicine, as that I had been given before had had side effects and prevented me driving. I don't take anything unless I am forced, as I can't bear being doped. Anyway, with Chita, I needed all my wits about me, all the time.

My reactions speeded up as I learned my dog; learned to outwit her on occasion. It began to be easier. If I saw a dog coming, I took evasive action; if I didn't then Chita won and leaped out and raved. She decided to adore Edith and had to be cured of leaping towards her or she dragged me over. If she saw another dog, the wild light shone in her eyes.

I thought I had imagined it, until one day the owner of her nephew asked me if I had noticed a wild light in *his* eyes. I hadn't, but I watched him and it was there. Neither of us liked it. She knew Chita and she wondered about her dog.

Then one evening I had a phone call from a total stranger, the owner of Chita's brother; she asked what Chita was like. I told her; her dog was the same and she was desperate. He went for every dog they met. Could I give her the name of the police dog handler and his phone number? I did, but I never knew whether she followed it up and I was told later the dog had gone; I didn't check. I didn't want to be involved with any more like Chita. I had asked my caller if she knew of any others in the litter. Her cousin had another brother who was not only unsafe with dogs, but with people too. It didn't seem to me as if it was entirely the owner's fault as I knew the struggle I was having with Chita. You needed experience to deal with dogs like her and few owners had it.

I was by now struggling, not only with Chita, but with her niece and nephew. I woke at night worrying about them, as the owner of the niece was too gentle for her dog and would have done far better with something else. She adored her but she also tended to treat the dog as if she were human, and dogs aren't human. She was afraid of hurting her by using the neck chain to control her, and I couldn't get it into her that dogs aren't made like us; their necks are quite different and the neck chain is no worse than the bit on a horse. It doesn't hurt the horse if adjusted properly and used properly. A correctly-timed neck check isn't at all painful, or all the dogs trained that way would scream their heads off, and they don't. They wag their tails, understanding this form of communication.

Winter was terrible. We were snowed in twice and could go nowhere. I booked in at a show and never got there; twice I couldn't even get to the dog club and had to ring round to tell people I was snowed in. Chita couldn't get out and about and was frustrated. She was even less easy to live with when frustrated.

One day I laid her a track in deep snow. I put on her tracking harness, which she loves, and off we went. Down went her nose to the bottom of each footstep, deep sniff, consider. "Yes, that's right." On and on, and as I had made about three-hundred footprints, it took her a long time to make sure each was mine and what she was hunting. She slept very well that evening.

There came a gap in the weather and I went over to present a cup to the police handlers I knew, which is one of my favourite annual assignments. I was invited to sleep in the visitors' flat at the big training centre. It proved a bit daunting, as my dogs went to the kennels and I was alone at the top of an enormous building, with the oddest noises. But the flat was very comfortable; I had a bath, made tea, and sat down and read, for once free of the need to take dogs out last thing.

At home my last trip every day was up our field with the dogs, one at a time, as I soon found that if they went out together, they didn't get on with the job but each went off hunting something on its own; or they had wild get-togethers that ended in trouble as Chita got too excited. I therefore made the most of not going out with the dogs last thing that night. I had presented the cup that day; and next day I was going tracking with those off duty. But to my dismay, I discovered Janus had howled all night in the kennels and set off every other dog. The police dogs were there and my dog was unpopular. Off we went, dogs in the van, on their rugs as usual, amusing everyone, but much easier than having them restive in a strange place. Their own smells reassure them; rug meant lie down and be quiet. Chita, in with the other two, was remarkably good, especially as there was a police dog the other side of the van – a dog guard between them.

Out we went into the middle of nowhere.

The young dogs tracked; there were three of them, all trained, not yet ready to go operational. To my delight they were nearly as noisy as Chita and screamed with excitement while waiting their turn. She yelled when she saw her tracking harness. Quick, quick, quick. It was exceedingly noisy and as well we were isolated. People might think we were abusing the dogs, instead of giving them extreme pleasure.

By now I had taken Edith's advice, and I did what everyone who trains dogs for competition only thinks impossible; I trained Chita for about three hours every day. Most dogs need ten minutes, but she was from *working* lines. A lot of it wasn't formal training; she would hunt for hidden objects on the field, do her jumps and scales, sometimes a track; a lot of heelwork and long long long downstays. Half an hour's work first thing, then later on another half hour; and in the afternoon out to the beach car park and on hour or sometimes two there. Chita could go right on, but I couldn't. Exercise didn't tire her. She *had to* use her brain daily.

Edith had shown us how to teach the really awkward types the trained dumb-bell retrieve. Chita was awkward about every new lesson and this one was no exception, so we did dumb-bell lessons endlessly indoors. I discovered an American method of teaching, using titbits; this has to be done exceedingly carefully or the dog waits for the titbit and still won't retrieve.

I hadn't realised it, but I was learning more with Chita than ever before. I had learned a lot with the other two; had gone into new worlds that had been totally alien to me; had ventured among breeders, which isn't easy for the non-breeder, as a few breeders consider pet owners are mugs to be fleeced, or fools who have dogs for the wrong psychological reasons. They are quite prepared to make money off them, and now I had the dog club running I was annoyed on occasion to find someone who had fallen for the old, old story.

"It was lovely and I was running it on but it's too big for showing. However, all its ancestors are champions so it's £120."

It is hard to make up a pedigree without champions in it; champions aren't dogs to be in awe of, sometimes they are champions because three people were bribed to put them up, though that isn't common; but it can happen. Scotland Yard is investigating dog shows right now. Sometimes people do one another favours; I put your dog up if you put mine up when you judge. Sometimes the judges just plain don't know their dogs. I was once judged in Obedience by a fifteen-year-old, which is utterly absurd. Judges need experience. Wisdom is also necessary and sense about dogs; and a good knowledge of people as well or they do the job badly. It is a major responsibility and shows are run for competitors, not for judges; though some seem to forget that and feel they are conferring an honour. We only have to stay away and not honour them by showing under them; lots of people don't realise that showing can be dicey. I pick my judges now and that doesn't always work as when a class is too big it is divided and there is a draw to see whether a competitor works under the judge entered, or under a reserve, who might be a first-time newcomer, asked only because no one better was available. The result isn't accurate as it isn't good judging. Luckily, the vast majority of judges *are* very good.

I found at this stage that my writing helped me with my dogs. I hadn't really ever thought about it, but a writer about animals must research. Writing about farming and dogs, there are new ideas to learn about; always new people to meet. Over long years of talking to people, I have learned to identify the true professional; the top dedicated man or woman who knows his or her facts, who cares more about the truth and about doing the job to the best of one's ability than about showing up in a bad light. The true professional is prepared to scrap every theory and start again, without fear or favour, without thinking of anything except getting the right answer, even if it's not the answer he had hoped for.

My father used to say, "There are those who know. There are those who know they know. There are those who don't know. There are those who know they don't know. There are those who don't know they don't know but are certain that they do know. They are the most dangerous of all."

Having Chita made me look deeply into people, hunting for those who had the information that could unlock the door to her future. Having Chita made me see many in a different light; some of them were totally helpful, totally trustworthy, willing to share the knowledge they had. Others had their own needs and desires. For them *I* might be a doorway; wanting to know me for reasons other than myself and my dogs; wanting me to help write a book, introduce them to my agent, be able to boast that they knew me and had helped me, not because they wanted to help, but because through me they might gain a higher status. Or, I might lead them to something better than they already had.

It did them little good, as I have never trusted fame or publicity; neither have value except for a little while. People forget what they read last year. Death comes to everyone and, in the ending, what matters is not what they say you did, but *what* you did. My father dying said, "I am not afraid. I haven't harmed anyone knowingly," which to me summed up what life is about.

I am always safe with my dogs. They don't care who I am or what I am. With them, I never have to pretend, be polite, or act a part that is alien to me. I have often spoken in public, but unless I am with children I am never happy in the speaker's role. If I have my dogs with me, then I can relax. They want nothing except food and shelter and, most of all, to be wanted for themselves. They enjoy living to the full; they enjoy every moment of life, without fear for the future or regret for the past. They have opened a world to me that I would never have entered without them; a world that few share, because there are very few who think deeply enough about it. The human race is part of the animal world, but has become so arrogant it has destroyed its own sanity and life for many is totally pointless.

Everyone has different needs. For some, the world of dogs is a world in which breeder vies with breeder for championships; aims to produce a better-looking dog than the next person, a dog that conforms more nearly to a picture-book ideal.

For some, the world of dogs is the road to the top of Cruft's. In Obedience, to win the highest award in the country for the best-trained dog; the dog that makes fewest mistakes as it embarks on a routine set down long ago and faithfully followed. Though in the twenty years or more since it first started, a great deal more has been found out about dogs and how to train them; of how to work with them happily so that every dog has a chance of living a fuller life, a life that gives the dog purpose, instead of idling its time away lying by the fire, with an occasional walk and a daily meal thrown in to keep it exercised and alive.

For many of us, the world of the dog is the one way in which we can live as man was intended to live, a natural life in a natural world, where the beasts that are part of our inheritance have their part to play in our lives – man and animal have worked together for centuries. Only in the last fifty years has man begun to live in a totally alien urban environment – and many hate it.

For some of us, the world of training shows the way to control all dogs; without training, they remain wild, uncivilised and often nuisances. The ways of training are many. There is no one way to train a dog. I soon found with my puppy class I had to consider the pup; consider whether it was bold or timid, happy or cowed; consider where it lived. The needs of a dog in a town are different from those of a dog in the country. One may never see a sheep in all its life; another may meet them daily.

Mine will walk through a field of sheep now without turning a head, but I never have them off lead near stock; and I never, in the lambing season, take them, even on lead, anywhere near lambing ewes. A ewe may be frightened by the mere sight of a dog, even though he is leashed, and run and drop her lamb prematurely.

A good ram lamb can fetch as much as £3,000 in a top quality herd. Have we, just to exercise our dogs, any right to threaten the farmer's investment? There are other places to walk. If your dog is off lead, how does the watching farmer know that that dog is with you and is safe with his stock? He can't know, and he may shoot. I have known two dogs die, running through fields while their owners walked in the lane, unaware that those farmers had lost so many sheep worried by dogs that they shot first and asked afterwards.

Anyone who has seen a ewe with her guts torn out and her throat ripped open, while she is still alive, will be very careful where they walk even the safest dog.

Only last week I went down to the farm to train my dogs. They never did get trained, as a spaniel and a

Labrador were running among the chickens. I ran for the owner of the hens, and he caught the pair as they ripped a still warm and flapping bird apart. Two more lay dead and three were in the wood, having flown in panic over the fence. Some of the others were lacking feathers and were badly shocked. We went elsewhere, to let the survivors settle.

Two pet dogs, small, gentle, out for a walkabout, but in ten minutes they had done as much damage as a wild fox.

I had to work on Chita until she dropped fast, on command. 'Down, Chita, down,' and down she went, to lie till I reached her and put on her lead and stood beside her.

That was the goal I had to aim for. I knew a good deal more about training pups from Charlie's course, and had Janus been younger could undoubtedly have sharpened him up to at least winning that elusive First. But Janus was too old for competition, and Chita as yet a long way from beginning. I have never had any illusions about winning Cruft's. That was never my aim. I would have liked to have gone further with Janus; I could have done so prior to 1976, but once the rules were changed we were caught by them.

Too many were caught, and the rules have changed again, so that after May, 1980, it will be possible to work your dog in any class, and not have to win your way out of the nursery. It is much too late for Janus. He is an old dog now and his ring days are in the past. It wouldn't be fair to try, except perhaps at a tiny show for fun; not making him work if he didn't choose to.

All I wanted with Chita was to get her under control and perhaps qualify her in Working Trials. Control in fact with her meant far harder work on my part than it would for any easier dog. Something far beyond the requirements of either Trials or Obedience. She had to learn to be utterly reliable, totally obedient, and to overcome her own excitability. It was quite a task. She did, in our last club competition, take an easy First and win a cup. I had help then and trained Chita with the rest of the top class. Now, as sole trainer, I don't compete any longer. I had hoped to go much further with my new pup in competition but I doubted if she was the right type for Obedience at all. I needed very different breeding for that; and even then I could be unlucky as no breeder produces perfect dogs. If they say they do, they are liars. Many are excellent but there is not a dog alive that does not have some fault or another.

I had now collected an enormous number of friends at a distance, all helping me with advice.

Having met Edith and Bob and been reassured that it was definitely my dog and not me, I was feeling a little happier; the thought that possibly I had turned Chita into the lunatic she was, wasn't nice.

I was writing for the Alsatian League magazine, and through that someone told me of a half-brother of Chita's belonging to a police-dog handler; a man who had plenty of experience with dogs of all kinds, but with this he had had immense problems. The dog was so dominant that one day they came to a major confrontation. The policeman did win but he had to battle to win, and no one had seen anything quite like it before. I never did manage to find out exact details of that, but if a police-dog handler had major problems with a relative then I wasn't doing too badly with Chita. She was much calmer at home now and she mostly behaved in club; though one thing she hated was meeting other dogs unexpectedly when out. She *was* beginning to show signs of being trained and, if things went wrong, I could talk to Edith who was reassuring, though I now know that in private she and Bob did not think I would ever civilise Chita.

As Edith said, they didn't know me at that time. Most people take a year of knowing and nobody ever knows another person really well.

Appearances are deceptive. Lots of people seem to think I am milk mild and very genteel, a description that makes me laugh, as the people who apply it haven't ever really met me! They may have judged me for five minutes in the ring or seen me briefly over a cup of coffee. But you haven't written more than thirty books and over a thousand articles, and competed in a world that is very tough indeed by being genteel! I do have one firm rule though, I'll have nothing whatever to do with dishonesty. And I do try to help others when I can and to be understanding of other people's problems, though sometimes if people don't give you enough information you can make mistakes through lack of knowledge. I find some people think one can thought-read!

Through Chita, I had ventured into yet another part of the dog world that I had never expected to enter. Years before, I had started with Janus at dog club for the first time; ashamed of my dog, embarrassed because he too had been uncontrollable, and here I was nine years later learning with an even more difficult dog, and, at the same time, being involved with a club that I had started.

It was annoying to find yet another difficult dog. I could never be quite sure it *wasn't* me. I was seven years older than when I first had Janus. Then I went to Okehampton and met Chita's half-sister in the hands of someone who had worked for many years in top competition and who'd re-trained sheep killers. She said her bitch was the only one she'd ever had who charged into dog club on her hind legs – and who had to be chained in the kitchen so that she didn't (very happily and without any ill intent) destroy her surroundings. So it wasn't *me*.

I had never expected the club to last, let alone grow. It ran very well, as there were a number of people who joined at the beginning and who came regularly. We had very few activities. Should we do a display? I'd put it to the members and get their answer. Should we buy a dog for the Blind? We started the fund and organised a committee to watch over its growing. It has reached over £300 in seven months; however, we've another £700 to go as yet and it won't be easy to achieve our target.

At first the club was harassing in that I had no help. One or two people from other clubs helped on occasion, but they had a long way to come and I couldn't ask them to stay, or to fight against the awful summer traffic that completely chokes our roads.

I arranged chairs, took the money, took details of new members and taught as well, which proved far from easy. I asked for volunteers and got three, who then helped with shifting around the furniture and taking the money. One of them volunteered to look after the accounts, but got tired of it and gave them to someone else. The same person offered to take one of the classes, but one week she was very late and the next not there at all, so that didn't work either.

People who take on responsibilities must be reliable.

We decided that the club, which had trebled in numbers in three weeks, was now likely to go on, and we applied for registration with the Kennel Club. We organised a committee to run it and sorted everything out, so we knew what we were doing; we haven't yet heard whether our application has been accepted. It is anything but easy to go from twenty members to nearly sixty in so short a time. It meant that instead of having dogs at all stages, as one does in an established club, almost all our dogs were brand new to training and it was necessary to be rather hard on people to ensure there were no fights due to the dogs being too close and annoying one another.

There was a major disadvantage in that Chita could never be trained in class, so I had to go over to Edith, or not train her with help at all. Chita and I both needed help and it is never easy to work entirely alone. Now, months later, someone has joined the club who can teach the top class and Chita will be trained there; and I will be free of the need to drive a round trip of eighty miles to teach her, much as I enjoyed doing it. It wasn't easy for either of us to fit it in.

Chapter Eight

Edith's Instructor's course was held in March. It had been a bitter winter; we had been snowed in twice and the weather never seemed to let up. Out of doors was misery; walking by the sea soon taught me why the locals never went near the beaches. The sand blew into our eyes and the dogs came out of the car, stood facing the wind and got straight back in again; more sense than I!

Walk on any road near the beaches and the wind threatened to take our breath away; the sea was grey and dismal; and at low tide miserable groups of swans huddled together, their feathers ruffled, their attitudes dejected. They even ignored the dogs.

The garden was windswept, the fields bleak and our neighbour drove three times daily with loads of hay for the sheep and cattle. He lambs late, which is as well, as this year the death toll was high. All kinds of diseases claimed the babies, born into a grey dismal world of bitter frost and icy winds; of snow and of constant rain. Our vet was always out, and always weary.

Wind and rain; everyone we met seemed edgy and irritable. The dogs didn't enjoy exercise and I didn't enjoy taking them. Most of Chita's training was done indoors. Much of the time it was too cold for her to jump; the ground was rock hard and she would have been jarred as she landed. We couldn't make much progress.

I was to stay once more at the hotel. My little room by now was familiar. They still had the electricians in, working, and the power in my wing was still off. So I was given the Calor gas stove and two hot-water bottles this time and was probably more comfortable than anybody.

All training courses are fascinating. Who is there? What sort of people? What sort of dogs? What are we going to do?

Someone else was taking the club for me; it was the first

Tuesday I had had off teaching since starting six months before, except for two weeks at Christmas. It seemed odd not to be at club on Tuesday night. Meanwhile, it was Saturday night and everyone was warily summing up everyone else. We were going to spend seven days in close company. What kind of people were we? I was older than most, though one member was definitely older than I, and she had an even older friend with her who was nothing to do with dogs. The rest were sharing caravans. I won't share, not with three dogs. I need to be alone, as I may have an article to write when everyone else wants to talk or sleep and I don't want to lie frustrated or disturb other people. My little room here was a haven, a refuge I could escape to on my own.

Bob and Edith do thorough preparation. I soon saw that we were in for a much more gruelling time than I had ever had before on this type of course, as we had much ground to cover in one week. We were to go out better equipped to instruct than we had been before, or they would know the reason why.

I began to feel totally lost, as everyone else seemed so much more competent than I was. They had all been instructing others for years; I had only been doing it for a short time. They were all competition minded; I am a bit half-hearted over that, as to me control of the dog is far more important than precision in the ring.

My dogs would undoubtedly be the worst dogs there, as Chita was still so uncontrollable that I was thoroughly ashamed of her. No one would understand my problems with her.

I sat in the bar, watching other people, knowing one person only there, who I had met before and who, I then discovered, was as much at sea as I was and feeling equally at a loss. Neither of us was working top Obedience; everyone else sounded so glib about their dogs, about the shows they had entered and the judges they had had, the points they had lost and the classes they had won. We spent a lot of the week together and she helped me later, but was defeated by the traffic problem.

The first lecture was on the need to present one's instruction clearly to a class; to think about instructing from the instructor's viewpoint; to be clear, audible, precise, neatly dressed (not as surprising a stricture as readers might think as some dog people tend to be remarkably scruffy). We were to make sure that, outdoors, the sun wasn't in folk's eyes; that the exercise was clearly demonstrated. I was weltering in a sea of facts.

They then did a playlet; a dog club as it should be and a dog club as it shouldn't be, with no one interested, dogs barking and misbehaving and fouling the floor (though they didn't act that bit, only mentioned it). I made a firm memorandum to myself to ensure that we had a few people who would talk to newcomers, would be very strict about fouling, and that I should always be there very early and very neatly dressed though you can't avoid a few dog hairs. Trouble is, if I go early, someone always seems to beat me to it and the evening starts earlier than I intend. I have learned since then to be firm about that.

I knew I was going to have problems with Chita once I brought her out, though after another handling weekend in February I now had a bit more control. My hands were so sore and swollen that it hurt to hold her, and hurt more to correct her. I cursed the fact that she had decided to adore Edith as well as me, and that if she saw Edith and I didn't, she lunged towards her and I almost fell.

So we had to do anti-Edith training, which was a bore. Chita knew when I was ready for her and didn't lunge; she knew when I wasn't concentrating and then again she had me off my feet, or nearly. I could have throttled her cheerfully at times. My only consolation was that many club dogs adored me as much as Chita adored Edith, so obviously they went for someone they felt bossed their owner.

There were twenty people on the course, many with more than one dog. I had always noticed that on handlers' courses, and at shows, a few people just aren't dog minded. They let all the dogs riot together, although they are supposedly training them. I had learned the hard way;

you can't train dogs that are allowed to play the fool. The professionals never let their dogs run free, on any occasion. If off lead, they are under total control. I had been too much among competition people, a few of them careless of dogs and of other people's problems; so taken up with winning and competing they never stopped to think. I do know handlers who have their dogs under total control, however, and one in particular is noteworthy for walking four dogs at heel, off lead, through a show, all of them behaving. People think she is showing off; she isn't. She is being professional.

I remembered the gamekeepers I knew, with their Pointers, never allowed to race off; the farmers with their collies, lying quietly waiting for a signal while boss is busy; the men who shoot, with dogs that must stay down as no one knows when a bird will rise and a gun go off; it could shoot the dog. Not all people who shoot are disciplined. Some dogs come out of the car like maniacs. I wonder what they do in motorway service stations? My dogs must always stay in the car when the boot is raised and not come out till told. Since Chita wouldn't learn, she used to be chained; if she hadn't been chained, she would be dead. One of my club members and her dog were attacked last week by a dog that leapt from a car. And a dog roared out of another car recently at a service station and attacked an innocent bystander: you can't be *too* careful with dogs.

"Very dangerous," said one of the handlers, seeing Chita's crate. It was an odd remark, but her feelings were echoed by one or two of the others. They obviously had never met a dog like Chita, and equally obviously, by their superior attitudes, they thought it was me, not her. I knew they were wrong so that didn't bother me much, but I wondered how on earth they managed to teach others when they knew so little about dogs or dog management themselves. I soon found out that some of them only had experience with one or two dogs.

I found out something else too while I was there. The people who did well were interested in *all* dogs, in all types of dog, in training any dog that came to hand and in discussing dog and owner together; they studied all dogs, not only their own. Those that did badly were interested occasionally to the point of total boredom, only in themselves and in their own dogs. Talk to them, and you could sit and listen to an endless screed about their dogs; nobody else's dogs; if *you* talked, they didn't listen. They interrupted, back again to their own pet and its problems and how to get it to win in the shows, never mind the dogs that people came to them with, for help, trusting them to know better; they just didn't care.

It shocked me to think that so many people in this country are trying to train others, for reasons that don't bear inspection, such as wanting to hire a hall for their own dogs and for getting better in competition themselves, not sharing their knowledge.

Many people never realise that if they teach a club they must never teach in front of their own dog. The dog lies there hearing master's voice go on and on, on and on, giving all sorts of commands. Dogs to the 'down'. A dog stands, bewildered and then goes down, doubtfully, but the command didn't apply to him; next time he will ignore it, and next time he might be in the competition ring. One dog shouldn't be trained in front of another, as the watching dog learns only to ignore commands.

Some let their would-be champions run wild before a show; out of the car, and they pelt round like lunatics, taking all the edge off their keenness; misbehaving, not coming when called, often arguing with another dog, and the owner then can't think why the dog won't behave later. Why should it? It never knew whether it was able to run riot or had to work sensibly; a dog can't differentiate. If a dog is to behave at shows, it needs to do so all the time or it may riot in the ring, for it's been rioting there before and one piece of grass is just like another piece of grass.

Insist one time and laugh another and you have lost the battle at once; a dog only understands total consistency.

It was going to be a very odd week. A very mixed bunch of people, all thrown together. Some knew each other already and belonged to the same club. They tended to go off in groups; some, being older, did try to mix with everyone, but it wasn't always easy. It was bitterly cold outside all the time; and by Monday I knew two things; I was developing both 'flu and lumbago and that was not at all funny.

We worked, out on the field, in the cold, the mountains snow-clad in the distance. The barren trees bleak; the wind and the rain always with us. Chita was her usual infuriating self, lunging to Edith, and even to Bob, who took her off me again and gave her a sharp lesson. I put her away and brought Janus or Puma, because I hadn't the energy, with a back that hurt all the time, or the strength to pull in this little rogue, and didn't she know it. Like a child that knows when its mother is off colour and plays up, Chita knew too. Children are basically animal and haven't lost their nearness to nature, which is probably why they act like young animals at times, very like them in behaviour.

Most people are basically shy in strange company. Courses are easier in that everyone has the same interests, and by Sunday evening people were able to discuss the day's training and talk to one another about their own dogs.

By the Tuesday we were all relaxing, realising others were in the same boat as us, not really knowing a great deal but desperately anxious to learn. We were also sorting ourselves out, so that I wanted to find people who knew more than I did and whose brains I could pick; they were welcome to pick mine.

I wanted information on puppy classes, which I was running; how to improve teaching all the time; how to make people *want* to train their dogs, interested in training their dogs, get results from training their dogs, without it being an awful chore.

A well-trained dog is such a pleasure to own; no headaches with him. He comes if you want him, lies still when you don't, never destroys your property. No dog is born like that, it is the training that does it.

Some, like Chita, come worse than others; some more easily; there are no rules. There isn't a breeder in the country who can guarantee the way an eight-week puppy will mature, in any hands; nature doesn't work that way. There are families in which nine children turn out well and the tenth is a criminal; no one knows why, but it comes from long-forgotten ancestry, a wild streak that is inherited, as often as not.

The virtue of a dog course for dog people is that all sorts of people come with all sorts of dogs; you see the timid and the bold, the untrained and the trained, the bad specimen and the good; the wary and the watchful; the dog that overguards.

Chita was still very unhappy with other dogs. It was 'get off or I'll kill you before you kill me.' Now that she was full-grown, it looked terrifying. Yet she never in fact connected; she barked at a distance and didn't wade in, which gave me hope. I never let her run free with other dogs, even if they were polite! Those on the course didn't much like her; I had to watch her all the time and it was much easier to bring out Janus or Puma and work them and relax with them. They did as they were told and neither was aggressive.

It was mostly the older dogs that came out on that course. They wouldn't let me down. While I was trying to learn, I wasn't trying to control a brash baby with total inability to behave herself. Chita would leap like a salmon up a fall to kiss a face; loved people, Chita did, but other people didn't know that so it mustn't happen. Few realised that what she needed now was loving too; kneel beside her and she relaxed, leaning against you, almost purring. She produced an odd little crooning growl when I stroked her tummy or her chest; ooh, lovely! She flew at Edith, wanting to kiss her, her tail going like a little windmill, her body bent in submission, but people misinterpreted it so I avoided Edith. It looked too much like an attack! In fact, most dog-club trainers find that any dog they have handled greets them with enthusiasm. Many dogs in our club greet me in the same way. It is hard on the owner!

That week we all had a really horrible virus; sore throats, headaches and temperatures at night. Half the people on the course were walking round at half throttle. Concentrating was difficult, and for two days I would have preferred bed, but that wouldn't teach me anything. We had an oral exam on the Thursday, and on the Wednesday several of us were in trouble; one had to go to bed with chest complications (and the hotel coped magnificently). The liaison officer's main job seemed to be buying cough mixture and cold cures, and at coffee time and in the bar in the evening we all took teaspoons and the bottle of medicine went the rounds; we ended with whisky and lemon at bedtime.

I couldn't manage Chita at all; I was in despair. She knew I wasn't 100% and she played on it, acting in a really evil way. I began almost to loathe her. Blasted, beastly pup. She was making my life total hell at times, and this was one of the times. I knew what people thought. I was older than most and couldn't manage a dog for tuppence. But at least Janus and Puma didn't play up.

We had to work hard all the time and know the show regulations. How large is a scent cloth? How many scent articles should there be in a competition ring? How far apart? What is the minimum width of a ring; the maximum? How many competitors may a judge judge in a day? How do you cure a sheep chaser? How do you re-train a dog that is bored with retrieving and refuses to perform the exercise? How do you make your dog pay attention? How do you train a young puppy? When do you start puppy training?

It seemed to go on and on and on; so much to cram in. Other courses hadn't done nearly as much as this, most worked in the mornings only; but we worked in the morning, the afternoon, and had lectures during the evenings. One evening was free. I lay on my bed, stove on, reading my notes, the dogs lying beside the bed, even

Chita quiet and still, and wondered wearily if I would pass the exam.

Pass mark was 80%. I would never do it. I felt ghastly. If only I could stay in bed, if only I could breathe, if only my throat and lungs didn't hurt so much. If only it weren't so cold and wet.

Next day was beyond the pale and we worked indoors.

By now we were all edgy and a bit snappy with anyone who came to pick our brains. I found other people, if they had it wrong, were confusing me; I wasn't well enough to concentrate properly. I was going home; this was insane.

I didn't go home. I had more cough mixture and Edith suggested I save my voice; so I sat, by now adding really bad lumbago to my other miseries. I was so stiff I could only just move – very cautiously. I went to bed early and read all my notes. Tomorrow was the day of the oral. Our judges were a very well-known championship judge who had trained her own champions, and a police officer who trained the police dogs and handlers. That meant we did have to know our stuff, as these people were both professionals at the top of their tree. The police officer also judged championship classes and police-dog trials.

It wasn't going to be easy.

Twenty of us; two weren't taking the exam. One was ill and three were taking advanced. Fourteen of us in the end were taking the instructor's test. I thought of that 80% I had to get and wondered if it was worth even trying. I couldn't make it, could I?

Everyone was defeated and several more of us felt ill. By now another member of the party had had to go to bed and have a doctor to see her, but our first invalid was up, looking rather ghastly but determined to have a try at the exam. She had lots of guts, as she really was very far from fit.

I started feeling a little better and my voice was returning, though I felt slightly sick as a result of the cough mixture and various cough sweets I was sucking to try and keep my voice. I didn't feel sociable at all; I wanted to be left alone, to sit alone, and to think over what

I had learned, if anything. I was beginning to wonder if it had sunk in. My brain was whirling with partly digested facts.

Our group was the last to sit the oral. Others went in and came out, some happy and some depressed; we weren't allowed to mix. Those lucky ones who had had their test were free to go, to sit right away from the waiting queue.

We had had a written exam in the morning. The oral began just after lunch. Waiting seemed endless. My turn came about four. I was so nervous, I wondered if I could even speak. It was silly, it didn't really matter if I failed, but I was teaching in a club and it seemed to me to be a total confidence trick to pretend to knowledge I didn't have. Also, many of the others had been teaching longer than I had, and nearly all were much higher in Competition than I was. I was going to come unstuck on the Kennel Club rules, as I wasn't working the higher classes and it's hard to remember things you haven't experienced, though Janus is trained in all the advanced work.

I could answer most of the written paper but I had made two absurd mistakes; and I knew I had as soon as I handed the paper in. Too late by then, and anyway the test might not be right, though I hoped it was and felt it was. I had enjoyed it.

My turn came for the oral.

It wasn't however, an oral examination; it was a relaxed conversation about dogs. I was soon at my ease and, since I have had dogs round me all my life, and few of the questions were about the regulations, I began to enjoy myself. Did I teach? Yes. What sort of dogs came to the club? What problems did they have? How did I get over them? I had one or two invented ways of doing that which the others had told me not to mention as, though they work, they aren't what the old timers use. But I forgot, and found my questioners were very interested in my methods, one of them being to teach a young puppy to hold a paper tube so that he doesn't tear up paper.

By now I was feeling much better and for the first time began to enjoy the evening. My throat was improving and my headache had gone. My back wasn't so bad. We had a sort of mini-party with absurd games; charades with radio and TV programmes and films, which I managed very well till someone asked me to mime the Krypton Factor, and that threw me completely!

Next day was the practical exam, indoors if the weather was foul. I hoped for foul weather as it would be easier to use my voice inside. Others were suffering the same way and were croaking. Maureen was almost voiceless, so it was an enormous relief to find we were to be in the big barn. Outside in a wind my voice might well be blown away and I wouldn't be heard by the judges. For once we were glad of a vile day.

Bob and Edith by now were like two collies with a herd of reluctant sheep, and I suspect suffered more than we did, as when my club had a display to give in public I was in agony lest something went wrong that let *me* down as a bad teacher; it was far worse than just taking my own dogs in to a show. I had nine people to watch. My reputation was at stake. Let dogs misbehave, foul the display ring, have an argument; imagination ran riot, and I knew then what Bob and Edith went through; had they taught us well? How many would pass?

I had enjoyed the oral, talking about dogs; now it was the practical, and again I was late on the list.

I went in, as nervous as I had ever been. The questions I was asked I knew the answer to well, though I began one routine and realised as soon as I started it that I was wrong; I had taken a beginner class up into an advanced routine, the problem being that everyone there was only pretending to be a beginner and I knew their dogs were all well trained.

I shook myself into awareness and went on.

It was over.

The rest of the day was free. I walked the dogs, and went back to wash and change for dinner; evening dress, a slap-up meal, and speeches of thanks, and we had presents to give our instructors. The judges had comments to make; and the evening would end with giving out certificates. Everyone would get a certificate for attending; only those who had over 80% would get the coveted Instructor certificates, and these I knew would be well earned by any who got them. I had never been through such a gruelling week. Even if I'd been fit, it would still have been gruelling.

Our police officer told an involved and very funny tongue-twisting story about a man who drove a tanker. We had wine and we had the speeches, but we were all waiting intently for our final marks to be given out.

At last the time came.

Edith read from the bottom up and the people came forward who had failed to achieve the coveted 80% but had, all of them, over 70%, which on that course was quite something.

Name after name, but not mine. I had been overlooked.

They began on those with over eighty percent and still my name didn't come. I stopped listening, knowing very well that I had failed to get what I had come for; that Edith had either missed me out through kindness, not wishing to show me up, as I did, after all, write about dogs, or she had simply overlooked my name.

"Aren't you moving?" someone said.

Edith was looking at me, holding out a certificate. I went to get it and looked with total disbelief at the mark. 91%. I was second, and if I hadn't made those two idiotic mistakes in the written exam, both of which I knew were wrong before I went out of the room, I would have been top. I went back to my seat, somewhat dazed. Now I could relax, and go back to teach in our dog club with much more confidence. I had learned a great deal too.

We went to talk in the bar. Only six of us had passed, and without realising it we grouped together. It was the six people I would have picked out, as we rarely talked about our own dogs; we talked about the dogs that came to us to be taught. I had several that were a bit of a problem; one lovely Pointer that was over sensitive; a boisterous goldie, the huge Newfoundland, and a very timid Labrador bitch. The others had dogs like them in club, or dogs with problems of their own.

Bedtime was very late. The dogs had been fed and were asleep in our cars. I took Janus in first as Chita, on her own, still screamed; she had to come out in the middle; alone in the room she cried, and alone in the car she cried, and it was after 1.00am. A wet night and a cold night. Janus settled on his bed, which came in with him, and out I went for Chita. Taking her in, I met my landlady and we had a chat so I was a fair time. I put Chita in with Janus and went back to the car.

Puma had managed to open the door (she is good at car doors) and the car was empty. The driver's door was swinging open. As I had taken the other two out through the hatchback, I knew I hadn't left it that way.

No Puma. I called her, and nothing happened. How long had she been gone and where had she gone?

It was nearly 1.30am. No one about now, as the rest were in caravans. The hotel staff had gone; the door was open for me. It is always very late before Helen and Ray finish, as they clear up each night before they go to bed. They were still up, but invisible, probably washing glasses.

The sheep were lambing.

Acres of ground and where did I start to look?

I went, very miserably towards the front of the hotel, to go in and ask Ray if he had a torch. I had gone out of the back door, which was by the kitchen and led directly to the room I always had when I stayed.

There was Puma, sitting patiently on the front doorstep, under the light. Wasn't I ever going to come and take her to bed? She was being so good, statue-like, her eyes fixed on the door in front of her through which, she was sure, I must come in the end.

I called her softly and she came racing to me, tail going, head down, ears flat, but moving; hind legs bent, seal-like, pushing against me.

"I thought I'd lost you; why were you so long?" After

that, when I left Puma, it was always in a locked car.

Even so, one day at a show I saw two dogs running towards me, exactly like my two, as I exercised Chita. I glanced at the car; the door swung wide. I called my two idiots, who had come to find me. I'd forgotten to lock the door as Chita was desperate to get out. Now locking it is always the first thing I do, though my passengers think I am nuts; but they don't know Puma. She once let five dogs and herself out of the paddock at Bolton's Guide Dog for the Blind Centre. They had had dogs in that paddock for years, and no other dog had ever found out how to open the latch. Puma is very clever, except at work; or maybe she is clever at evading work!

Meanwhile, I had achieved one ambition. I had my Instructor's certificate and could go back feeling more able to teach, but well aware I knew so little and needed to know much more. A feeling which still becomes over-whelming every Tuesday night, as we now have sixty dogs and owners – and they *all* have different problems!

In the morning, as I said goodbye to Edith, she asked if I would like a day's help with Chita, more or less once a week, until we had got her controllable. I'd been over about once a month up to then. I was very glad of the offer.

Chapter Nine

Working stock.

Competition lines; Obedience lines.

— A dog that 'works' in the ring doesn't *work*; it is on show for, at most, ten minutes. A dog trained for the ring is trained for five minutes, usually a few times a day.

Never train for more than two minutes at a time, people told me. You will bore the dog.

A working collie is out on the hills all day; rounding up sheep, walking miles a day, tirelessly, effortlessly, for ever. When he is not working he is under control, lying waiting for a command from his master.

He is never running free doing what he will, which might be chasing rabbits or cats, perhaps sheep, even with a working collie, unless he is trained and taught and commanded.

A working police dog is either in the kennel or the van. Or he is being trained, not for two minutes, but for long periods. He is out on patrol; he may be tracking all night. Endurance, going on for ever, needing all the exercise in the world. A working police dog does not run free out of control, ever. A word from his owner and he is back again, on duty. Under command. A working dog.

Working lines.

Not competition lines.

Working lines.

Chita wanted to be on the move all the time; up and doing, never resting. She didn't like lying down, so she had to lie still as an exercise, not to rest. She slept with one eye open and one ear pricked, and if I moved or there was a sound anywhere, she was up, alert, while the other two, neither bred for work, were lying sleepily looking at her.

For goodness sake, what's up with her now? their expressions would say.

I wouldn't hear a thing.

Nothing to hear. I'd take my glasses off, or close my book, or move my hands. Chita would see.

I'd look at my coat lying on the back of a chair, or touch her lead; I'd finish my coffee and put down the cup. Was I about to go off, go in the car, do something?

Chita was a dog bred for *work*, yes, and I was denying her. Edith recognised that.

Chita needed, not exercise, as that simply didn't tire her, but training for very long periods; an hour at a time three times a day. Had I time? She needed to tire her brain. I understood that as I have that kind of brain. It must be occupied or I get moody and very irritable.

I would have to make time.

But I would also take my time doing it, as I wasn't at all sure; I had never met a dog needing that amount of training and Edith could be wrong.

Edith and Bob had done a lot of thinking about Chita. We worked; how we worked. We worked until I was exhausted and could only just manage to go on; but Chita was never exhausted. If I found I had to stop and rest, Edith took her, and she too had to battle. It wasn't an easy task, even with an expert, as Chita, when she put her mind to it, which she often did, was a formidable opponent. She had no desire whatever to co-operate with anyone.

The first lessons weren't even in Obedience.

Out came Edith's lovely red setter, Gail; biddable, trained, obedient, sensible, on lead, to meet us as we walked round the house.

Chita, meeting her unexpectedly at the corner, lunged and yelled.

Edith had shown me how to check; it wasn't easy as the timing had to be right, the strength had to be right, and Chita could read the muscles tightening on my hands, and be out and back before I had time to blink.

"Chita, *leave*." Yell and check as you had to get your voice above her screech of fury.

"Going to kill Gail."

Gail would look at her tolerantly, an adult bitch with a kind nature, and walk on.

Round the house again, and again and again. Reverse

the direction, so that I'd never know when Edith and Gail would appear. Then I'd walk beside them, Chita on her lead, me ready to check her at the slightest movement. Up and down the lawn, teaching Chita to walk at heel, to concentrate on me, to ignore Gail. To sitstay beside Gail and not turn towards her, putting the two animals closer and closer all the time, every time, until both bitches were almost touching. At the end of two sessions, Chita was used to Gail and out came Mick the collie, and we went through the same procedure, until Chita was staying 'down', with Gail one side of her and Mick the other. We had her walking at heel, with Mick playing the fool on his own running to and from Edith, running free around us, while Gail did her own long downstay within sight.

Over and over again, meeting the dogs on lead every time, from all angles; expected and unexpected. Occasionally Bob brought his rough collie, Sam, and we'd try the same procedure. Though Bob was only at the same stage in competition as I was, he knew a good deal about dogs.

It was long, it was slow, it was tedious, but it was beginning to get results.

Chita was still defying me, but the defiance became less as she slowly began to learn I wouldn't have it. I had to be on the watch all the time; my reactions had to be faster than hers and I speeded up. It would have been far easier if my hands hadn't been so painful. It was winter and an abominable winter at that.

Sometimes we worked down by the sea, at the kennels. The dunes hid the water and deadened the sound of the waves. Winter was bitter; there was always snow on the hills. Sometimes there was water on the ground, and we floundered in Wellingtons, but always, whatever the weather, we worked, often in teeming rain and high winds.

'Chita, heel.' She learned to walk at heel, watching me.
'Chita, watch.' Her head turned to me.

We practised daily at home; we practised when we went over to Edith. Always on lead, as off lead she was far from controllable; she ran off, full of herself, mocking us. She made me very angry, but I had to hide my anger, as no one who is angry will get anywhere with a dog.

Patience.

I practised it as endlessly as I practised her heel position.

'Chita, come.'

On the lead, she came, beautifully. As yet, she wasn't off lead, and there was no practising off-lead heelwork. She began to learn to hold the dumb-bell; to carry the dumb-bell, to bring it to me.

At home, we practised her jumps, at which she was now very proficient.

'Chita, over.'

She leaped at the clear jump, legs tucked beneath her, going fast and high. Over and down.

"Stay down."

She began to stay down.

Over the six-foot scale and stay down on the other side. She loved scaling and attacked it with all her might, going over it without any effort. She was very small and very light. A bitch of bigger build would have had more trouble.

She did that so well that at the police school, when I put her over the massive scale there, the sergeant and the inspector watched and said, "She won't do it. She's too small!"

"Want to bet?"

They didn't accept, which was just as well, as she soared over effortlessly, dropped, went down and on command returned. That at least she could do, and do very well.

Heelwork improved. Then came the day when she came, very briefly, off lead and stayed beside me, walking perfectly, sitting straight. I began to build on that; with Chita nothing could be done in a hurry, nothing could be done fast.

"How do you train a good dog?" I had said to Anne and Pat in Worthing when I was down there.

They'd both laughed and answered, "Slowly."

Not everyone would agree. Some want results fast, but

it's necessary to build gradually, especially with an animal like Chita, to make sure the basic knowledge is there in the dog, and the dog understands. One false move and the work is undone; one angry word and the dog stops co-operating. You can't train every dog at the same rate.

With Chita, it was always necessary to go slowly and to be absolutely sure she knew exactly what she was doing. For weeks, on the left turn, Edith told me to say 'back' to her, as I turned. It didn't work; Chita would pause and look at me puzzled!

"Stupid bitch."

It was totally exasperating.

Then, one morning, sending her over the scale, I listened to myself. Routine can become such a habit, you don't think about what you are saying.

"Chita, over."

"Chita, *back*."

Back didn't mean turning left; it meant going back after you had gone over the scale, so no wonder she was puzzled; I simply used the word 'tighten' after that and had no more trouble. So that was our fault, not hers. It doesn't matter what word you use so long as it's always the same one. It's the sound that matters – not the meaning.

She would still defy me.

Chita wanted a great deal, she wanted it fast and she saw no reason why she should change her mind. One afternoon I had her out by myself. The other two dogs were in the car and we were walking alongside a fence, beyond which were sheep. Normally she ignored them, but as we came towards the gate, the sheep scented her and bolted.

She flashed over the wall, through the wire, still on the lead, and was after them. I was spread-eagled, face against the wire, neck almost gashed, feeling the barbs, in such a position it was almost impossible to get at her.

I yelled.

She turned her head and I hauled her in fast. And as she came over the wall, I grabbed her by the scruff of her neck and shook her with all my strength. She was coming straight at me, snarling. She meant to attack me and she had to be stopped, and stopped immediately.

I lifted her in the air and flung her down on the grass and leaned on her with all my weight, holding her head against the ground as Puma had held her head in the early days. My coat was half off me, my scarf on the ground, as was my hat. I wasn't hurt but I was very angry; and briefly I had been frightened, as she definitely meant to attack. The wild light was back in her eyes and she had sprung at me, growling and snapping. I had stopped her doing as *she* wished. Had she gone, she'd have killed sheep.

I held Chita until she stopped struggling.

She wasn't going to get up until I let her up. I didn't know I had the strength but I had been both scared and angry. Had she succeeded in her attack, that would have been the end. She'd have had to be put down. She was, momentarily, out of her mind. She hadn't known what she was doing, and she hadn't yet been shown clearly, once for all, that I was stronger than she was. I should have shown her, long before, but it isn't easy to accept that you have to take such measures with any dog. Some people never do – and that's the end of a lot of dogs that might have grown into very good animals indeed.

I released her cautiously.

She stood up, shook herself and licked my hand.

She walked beside me, meekly, back to the car. She climbed inside without going for either of the other dogs. She dropped when I told her to drop, and I drove home with a small exhausted bitch lying absolutely quiet. From then on, the only sound she ever made was a normal dog-like whimper. Occasionally, if she were very excited, she might create, but she knew now that I was stronger than she was and that I could, if I wished, throw her off her feet as easily as Janus did. If I had watched *him*, I might have mastered her long ago.

Now she began to work for me. Heelwork improved immensely. She enjoyed working, and when the slip chain was brought out, jumped into it, eager to start, eager to please, a very different animal indeed.

She was still difficult to control, but I had learned that when she lunged, I could snatch the lead and could bring her flying back to my heels, surprised beyond measure;

but she only lunged when I was completely off guard. It's a knack, and dogs understand instantly. If she saw Edith, my hands only had to tighten on the lead and she changed her mind about running to her. Lunging stopped except on very rare occasions, and now I was ready for them.

She began to greet Kenneth with a good deal of affection and less inclination to puddle on his shoes, and he began to tolerate her. If she asked nicely, she was patted, as he sat in his chair.

Sometimes he would take dog biscuits from the box and have six in his pocket, two for each dog, and line the dogs up in front of him and offer them their goodies. Chita watched eagerly, knowing she always would get hers last. He had to be careful not to keep her waiting too long or she snatched, and when she snatched her teeth sometimes nipped, not intentionally but because she was too eager. She had to be taught so much.

At night she learned to lie quietly and behave herself, and now that we were working together I could tire her more easily and she'd relax instead of being ready to spring up, eager for movement, restless and unhappy at lying still. Her training began to be fun, instead of an ordeal during which I strove to master her and she outwitted me.

We walked. We did long downstays. We practised heelwork and heel positions, retrieve and recall; and I began to teach her the send-away to a mat. She'd run off from me and, when she reached the mat, drop down and lie there until she was called to heel again.

Each week I could add a little more interest to her training and she began to show an enormous amount of keenness, at one point being so eager to please she did everything too soon; and I had to teach her to wait until she was commanded, for anticipation loses as many points as not doing it at all.

We had no more trouble with sheep. She now accepted that *I* was boss; and she obeyed me. She came when called and I found she could be let out in the morning and would come in again immediately she had done all she needed to do. No more having to go outside with her; no calling her until I was angry and had difficulty in welcoming her when she finally decided to come. No more sessions on her long line, training over and over to come when called. Puma had always come fast; Janus never. He had to be told to 'fetch,' and then he would always come, the retriever in him dominant above all training.

Chita began to fetch anything I threw. She was beginning to search and beginning to track on my own tracks; she screamed with delight when she saw the tracking harness and had an infuriating habit of helping me put it on, so that she jumped into the first available neck gap. Unfortunately, a tracking harness is very complex and she invariably got her head into one of the leg holes, with the leather straps in an intricate tangle. Putting on her harness became more difficult than it need have been and, by the time I got the head buckles done up and she was safely inside it, both of us would be suffering from severe frustration and she would go off like a rocket, while I struggled to keep up.

Tracking was much more energetic for me than for her. I'd lay the track, walking over the grass, putting in stakes at intervals so that I knew where I had turned; I'd then return to the car and she'd follow the track on her long line; and when she had completed it and been rewarded, back she'd go in the car, while I went out to retrieve my poles.

I seemed to get ten times as much exercise as the dogs.

We practised daily, and went over to show Edith that we had been working and had improved.

I thought about training; wrote down her training; tried to improve on her training.

Not for prizes, not for personal kudos, but for sheer basic *control*. One day, it might all pay off.

It was very wearing.

It was maddening, as some days she was wonderful, and I'd begin to feel that at last we were making progress, that everything was worthwhile. Then, quite suddenly, she'd regress and seemingly forget everything I'd ever taught her.

It was a remarkably unrewarding way to live.

Chapter Ten

Training Chita.

It dominated everything. Not for shows; for impressing other people. Not for personal prestige. I was training her for life itself. Her life. It was balanced delicately against what I could do for her, because unless I did it, I had no choice. If she transgressed once, Kenneth would insist I put her down – and I'd agree.

No one can balance the life of a dog against human lives.

The trouble was that she had now fastened herself to my affections more firmly than I realised. She was exasperating, exhausting; at times her stubbornness was devastating, but in between, at home, she was totally my dog.

She slept at my feet; Puma slept in a corner; Janus on the hearthrug. She came to me always when in trouble of any sort, however major, however minor. Her small black mask would be looking up at me, a question in her eyes. Trouble was, I often didn't know what question.

Training.

I read books on training; I concentrated on getting control. Training. Control. It was like a train going over the rails, faster and faster, and if I didn't manage to get it right one day, it would go off the rails and my life would change again; this time for the worse because I would have lost all confidence. I would have given up, without even trying; I would never have known if this one really had beaten me, or if, had I persevered, I would have come out on top.

If I struggled with the dog and was defeated by disease, or perhaps she had a brain tumour, that was one thing; but if I gave up, I wouldn't be able to help the owner of her nephew; or the owner of her niece. I was more bothered about the nephew; he was big, he was strong and he was as wilful and difficult as Chita, and he was going to be twice her size. If she had been bigger I could never have gone on.

I had every incentive to go on. If only I weren't so tired, as I hadn't time to train for long enough to exhaust Chita. She exhausted me. Furthermore, she wasn't a pup any longer; she was eighteen months old. Maybe when she was two, three, or four, she'd mature properly, be a credit to me and not a menace to my peace of mind. Maybe she'd be a dog I could enjoy wholeheartedly instead of only at times, one I didn't regret having met; a dog that might even work well and win prizes. Training had to have some point, some goal, or I left it. With competition ahead, I worked.

It was stupid to dream. I needed to be hard-headed with this one. She wasn't nearly ready for shows; maybe she never would be. Other people could train their dogs and enter shows when the dog was less than a year old; I saw their looks of disbelief, knew of the things they said behind my back, through guesswork: "Joyce again with yet another dog she can't train. Funny, isn't it? You'd think by now she'd either have a decent dog, or would realise it has to be her. She always makes excuses."

At times when life is going badly wrong, you can't always see clearly; you are too busy coping with disaster. But if there is time to sit and think, to take a day off, to consider, then things can change and sometimes they change in the oddest way.

I knew while I was working with Edith that one of my main problems was my hands; I had to use a tool to get the top off even a sauce bottle, as there was no strength in them. My fingers hurt, my wrists hurt, and Chita's lead hurt, and the only way I could get power to check her was to use the lead in anything but the right way. I'd use my body with the lead behind it; use the lead round my forearms and use it hard. And my monkey knew it and took advantage every time.

I thought of all the advice I had been given. It wasn't much use if I couldn't manage the dog. But I couldn't sell her; it would be a mean trick to land someone else with her. Edith agreed with me. If I gave up on Chita, there was only one answer for her. An ignominious end in an incinerator, or buried in our field, a constant reminder of defeat.

That might well have been the end of it, had it not been for another set of events which, if put into one of my fictional stories, nobody would believe. But several people can vouch for the truth of this particular part of my book, though some took a long time in so doing!

The instructors' course was over, and I was back teaching in club. I had been over again to Edith, and it was nearing my mother's birthday, March 30th. She lived alone and we thought it would be nice if I could go down.

It had been quite a winter but winter was over, surely now. March 29th, 1979. I loaded my car with my gear for a week; packed case, and dogs, of course, with dog food and a six-and-a-half-pound pack of dog biscuits. I rang my mother the night before; I hoped to be down in Bexhill by about six. I would start early, very early.

It was dark when we set out and cold, but it was raining. No frost, no snow. I hate snow when I am driving. It terrifies me, as it is remorseless, falling endlessly, masking everything, a killer.

I had no problem at all until I reached Bethesda on the A5. Bethesda is high and sleet was falling, sleet containing large particles of snow. I set my windscreen wipers running. If I met snow, I would turn back. I had forgotten what the road was like.

A few miles further on I ran into snow. It had been falling for a long time and I was between stone walls, the cliffs on one side towering above me, the wall on the other side shielding me from a long drop and the snow deepening and thickening. The lights of a large lorry shone in my mirror. There was nothing in front of me, not even, rather alarmingly, tracks in the snow.

There was nowhere to turn. I couldn't stop, or I would be trapped; if I went on, I might be trapped. I turned on my radio, the only comfort in a world that was rapidly vanishing into whiteness.

The cliffs ended and we came out on to the moors; no landmarks; no way to tell if I was in the road, or in the ditch. The lorry overtook me, and the driver yelled that he'd break trail for me; I could drive in his tyre marks as he was heavier. It was a relief to have him in front; if he went off the road I would see and could stop.

Snow thickened and suddenly the windscreen wipers weren't clearing it at all. The world had gone. I was being buried. I turned up the radio louder and sat, watching my windows masked by snow. One of the dogs whimpered. I waited, and cautiously opened my door. The lorry was stationary too, the driver busy sweeping snow off his windscreen and windows.

I got out and swept the snow off mine.

The Citroen has three heights; I needed the highest to clear the hummocks he was leaving in the middle of the road. He lifted a thumb, got back in the cab and drove on. I followed, doing about three miles an hour. He was nosing down the road, obviously watching the humps at the sides, which might be walls, might be abandoned cars, might be anything.

We came to a tiny village; a few houses, and a shop. He stopped.

I stopped.

I got out.

"I'm turning here and going back," he said.

"You aren't, you know," said a voice behind me, and I found I had been followed by another car. The driver had joined us. "I tried that. The road's blocked in every direction."

I looked bleakly at my car. In the middle of nowhere, snowing hard and much more to come, and three dogs. What did I do?

We all went into the shop. It was cold and it was dark and the owner wasn't exactly happy as the power had gone off in the village at midnight and no one had any heat. I bought some chocolate and chewed it gloomily.

I had sandwiches and coffee in my car and it was almost eleven. I had travelled around forty miles in exactly five hours. I got into the car, where at least it was warm, drank my coffee and ate a sandwich. I could buy something in the shop to keep going.

I watched people going from house to house with teapots; someone must have had a primus stove. I looked at the houses. Warmth? Perhaps not; but shelter, certainly. If I stayed in the car we would get snowed in; and also what did one do for a loo?

I went back to the shop and bought some more sweets, as there didn't seem much point in buying anything in tins; I hadn't a tin opener. I couldn't ring my mother; the phone apparently wasn't working.

Someone came into the shop, and I asked her rather forlornly if she knew where I could find shelter. Was there a pub within reach? The road was still passable, just, for a little way further.

I could come up to her farmhouse. She and her son had both intended travelling, she to Aintree to the races, he back to university in the north. They had had to turn back.

"I have three dogs in the car."

She had three dogs too. Mine were safe, weren't they? I thought of Chita, who had been behaving well for about two weeks and hopefully said yes, praying I wasn't going to be proved a liar. I was scared silly, standing there with the snow falling, my car slowly being covered, and the dogs inside.

We put them on their leads and took the biscuit pack. One dog each. I took Chita, my hostess took Janus and her son had Puma; but, as Janus seemed to have gone 'high' with the snow, they swopped. My little fiend hadn't seen snow like that before; she plunged, lunged and cavorted, full of puppy madness, delighted to be alive and, as always, twenty times as enthusiastic as any other dog.

Along the slippery road, the snow now more like hail, a bitter wind flinging it into our faces, our heads down, the dogs pulling. Why on earth did I have dogs? They really did complicate life. Through a field gate and up the mountain. Up and up the mountain, floundering knee-deep.

To add to the fun, there were sheep, miserable and huddled, and they came towards us, which didn't help at all with the dogs.

It was now a grim struggle against wind and weather and once or twice I wondered how high we were going and where the farmhouse was.

The snow soaked the biscuit bag and it broke. Three dogs pounced on the bounty lying there, choking down biscuits as if they had never been fed. It took all our strength to get them away for they hated leaving the food behind but we couldn't stay there. The last we saw of the biscuits was that the sheep were interested in them, nosing them forlornly. I wondered if they would eat them; they hadn't much else to eat.

By now it was agony just walking; we were wet, we were cold, and the stinging wind was bitter; an Arctic wind from the Siberian plains. I had never experienced anything like it. I had visions of being snowed up here for weeks.

The farmhouse appeared, totally covered in snow; we ploughed through the yard. Somewhere there were chickens. The dogs greeted us but were taken upstairs and we went indoors, mercifully out of the wind, but they too had no electricity and the only heat came from two tiny paraffin stoves. We sat in our overcoats in the dining room, like refugees. The dogs settled down, rather forlornly.

Snow drifted down, masking the windows.

It was possible to make coffee. We drank coffee and introduced ourselves. My hostess was secretary of a club that helped disabled children learn to ride. They had an Annual General Meeting that night and she had to phone about twenty people at least to pass on messages saying there wouldn't be a meeting as a tree was down across the road that led to their meeting place and, even if the snow cleared, the tree couldn't be moved till next day.

The phone had developed a very odd fault; she could

phone all numbers above 5 and none below, so her list became complicated as she worked out who she could ring and who could then get through to the next person. The day wore on, endlessly for all of us.

I read a copy of a magazine; her son worked on drawings of clocks which he made, most beautifully; the dogs slept.

We ate the picnic that had been intended for Aintree. Soup, a superb quiche and sandwiches and coffee.

At about 2.30pm the phone rang. It was the village shop.

The snow plough had got through from Bettws y Coed. I could get back to Anglesey, but not on to Llangollen, as the road was now blocked in a major way.

I had rung through to Kenneth, who had found it hard to believe I was snowed in. It was still raining where he was.

We struggled down the mountain, complete with three dogs, who discovered the sodden remains of their biscuits and grabbed a quick mouthful. The snow had been melting fast and we walked in rutted gullies, up to our knees in water. The dogs ploughed down the rushing stream, shoulder deep, Chita wettest of all as she was smallest. I did have towels in the car.

We got down to the road and I changed my socks and trousers. I couldn't find spare socks but I had dry fur boots which at least were warm; and the car heater would work; if the car would start. Most of the other cars that had been lined up beside me had gone and so had the lorry.

I dried the dogs as best I could and thanked my hostess, not knowing quite how to do it properly, but I had several of my books in the car and I gave her those.

Then, looking at my hands, which were by now looking and feeling like raw blue meat, she said, "You need my sister's healer."

I looked at her. I didn't really believe in healers, never having done more than read about them, but she wrote down the address. I took it, intending to do nothing whatever about it. I tucked in into my purse, and she told me about her sister who had been semi-crippled and was now riding point-to-point again.

It sounded a wonderful story, but I was too cold, too wet and too worried about my return journey to take it in.

The car started in the end and we nosed out onto the road, the smell of soaking wet dogs all pervading. I glanced behind me. They were all huddled close, as I hadn't put Chita in her cage, thinking she needed as much warmth as she could get and hoping she would behave. They were lying quietly, watching me. I felt I had a lot of responsibility; if I crashed the car . . .

Out into the road and back towards home, the snow amazingly melted; the road was a bit slippery and the fields and hills were white, but that was all.

The heater was working well now, and I switched on the radio. It was then almost 3.00pm. I would be home by five at this rate and could get really warm and dry and have a meal.

I drove down the gentle incline and turned the corner and ran straight into trouble. The snow plough had only been along in one direction and not two. Here the snow was deep, was rutted, and was freezing hard. I drove, when I could see, on the wrong side of the road, having to slide back into the ruts when something came in the opposite direction. I was crawling and slipping at about two miles an hour, nosing along in first gear, the car slithering horribly. I was clutching the wheel and praying for all I was worth. The sides of the road were humped white lumps; ditches, or drifts, or buried sheep, or buried cars. At one point the road swept off into nowhere, a thick fog obscuring everything.

My arms ached with holding the car on the road. I dared not stop in case I couldn't start again. It was fine when I had a long view and nothing coming, but I had to be sure I did have a long view and could get back onto my beastly ruts again, and jerk along, the wheel sliding unnervingly. I was never above second gear.

The songs the radio sang were wildly inappropriate.

The dogs were angelic, not moving, not making a noise. I could see Puma in my mirror, she always lies with her head slightly raised looking out of the window.

Three hours later I came on to a stretch of clear road, pulled into a lay-by and looked behind me. Chita was curled tightly between the other two, her head on Janus's back; they had dozed off and seemed warm enough. I had some coffee left and some sandwiches and stopped to recover, and eat. My hands hurt horribly, as like a fool I had forgotten my gloves and left them in the car when we went up the hill to our rescuer's home, and they hadn't recovered from being so wet and cold.

My arms ached and my jaw ached; I'd been driving with my teeth clenched. Looking in front of me, it was hard to believe we had just driven through such a scene. There was no snow at all ahead.

I drove down to the next village and stopped to buy some chocolate.

"Where did you come from?" the shopkeeper asked.

I told him.

"But the pass is still closed; the snow plough hasn't come back. No other car has been through. What was it like?"

"Hell," I said, and was believed.

It was very good to get home. Never again would I try a wintry journey as both roads are liable to close. Two years before I had come back from the Lakes, where I'd been to a book show in a school, with the two older dogs, and had been re-routed when only thirty miles from home; the road was blocked by snow ahead. I had to go back along the coast; nowhere was open for tea; the car slithered on snow and ice, and a policeman had to knock up a garage and get me more petrol as I hadn't bargained on an eighty-mile detour.

I had visions of a car in the ditch and myself and the dogs dead of exposure, and it wasn't funny. This second journey had been even worse.

I rang my mother, who was very disappointed. They had no snow but she did understand and once more spent her birthday on her own, though my sister, who is a theatre sister in the hospital there, always goes in after work on our mother's birthday; and my other sister makes a point of going over too if the weather lets her. It would have been nice to be there, but not in weather like that. We would wait till June; surely it wouldn't snow then.

I managed to go over to Edith, but my hands were so painful I didn't do much good; I couldn't check Chita, I had no power in my hands at all. I couldn't even unscrew the lid of a jampot. I would have to get rid of the dogs.

I was not going to get rid of the dogs. Come hell or high water, no matter what, I was going to try everything in my power to get my hands right.

I looked out that piece of paper. I looked at the address. It was about two hundred miles away from me. How could anyone help at that distance?

Orthodox medicine doesn't help rheumatism and I don't like the drugs they use. I had had one which had produced side effects; another which had meant I couldn't drive, and neither had done much good. They allayed the pain but did nothing for the deformity or the lack of power in the muscles.

I wrote to the address I had been given.

Two days later I found myself exercising my hands uncontrollably, as if they were being manipulated by someone else. I tried to stop, but every now and again flexed my fingers and bent them again. I put my hands behind me. I was conscious of my hands, of a terrific need to move them, to make the fingers work, to bend them and clench them.

It was silly.

It happened again on the next night. It was a weekend and I found myself totally hand-conscious. On the Monday morning I got a letter saying the healer would take me on; and that healing was done by radiasthesia, by healing radiations. You can't see light waves, sound waves, radio or TV waves; or what makes the telephone work or electricity or magnetism; so why not healing waves? Something was making me use my hands far more than usual.

I found they were easier, the pain was less. And then, not believing it at all, I found the swelling of the knuckles was going down and the blueness vanishing. It was happening as I watched, every day making a change. I didn't believe it; I couldn't believe it. It was too good to be true; but I couldn't tell Kenneth, he'd laugh. In fact he learned of it through my mother a year later – and he didn't laugh. She did! He'd seen my hands.

I said nothing for several weeks and then told Bob and Edith. Edith gave me an odd, old-fashioned considering look and said nothing. Bob laughed.

A few weeks later, he came in while we were lunching. I hadn't seen him since I had mentioned my hands.

"Let's see those wonderful hands of yours, Joyce," he said, with a grin that said he knew I was a fool and now I would have to own up.

I spread my hands out. The fingers, except for the middle finger of each hand, were reduced to normal size, all swelling gone; mobile, the power coming back. I could snatch Chita's lead and it didn't hurt. The colour was normal; they were almost back to what they had been when I was much younger and I found myself looking at them, night after night, not really believing it was possible. Yet now, a year later, all swelling has gone. The scar from the cut due to Chita's impatience is gone, just a thin white line instead of a cobbled-up mass of badly healed tissue, and I can once more wear the wedding ring I had abandoned as too small ten years ago, when it was cut off.

"Bloody hell," Bob said. "They are better."

Bob and Edith watched them change from being nearly crippled, so badly that Edith thought I would have to give up the dogs, to being back to normal, so that I can take dogs in my club belonging to people younger than I am and use far more power than they have.

I don't pretend to understand, but that doesn't make me any the less grateful; in fact I don't know what I would have done if my hands had got worse, because I couldn't bear to be without dogs, and without the dog club I would have lost a great many new friends and a great deal of invaluable experience that I can get in no other way.

It was an odd chain of events; the journey I never completed; the farm house I visited briefly; the casual mention of something I didn't even believe in. And the follow-up.

Today I am fitter than I have been for years as there is a bonus to good hands; I can go out in all weathers, can train Chita and toughen myself up; and through her I have a new life in so many directions that, in spite of all I have endured through her, I know that without her I would not be the person I am today. She has changed me, because I had to change her.

It is extraordinary to think that events follow in a chain, and years later you can trace back to the links; apparently disconnected, but all, if you learn to take circumstances that seem to your disadvantage and turn them into your advantage, can make an enormous difference to your life.

In some ways, it is chance; but chance has to be recognised and it's necessary to try and make capital out of disasters. I have gone deep into dog training, and with it has come the knowledge that I do know a great deal more than many other people, but also the awareness that however long I live, I will never know enough. Nobody knows enough.

The next dog will teach me all over again; it will be nothing like the three I have now.

Meanwhile, once my hands were better, life opened out again; and began to get exciting. My brain worked better and, with Chita behaving herself well at home, I finished two books, *The January Queen*, about a Shire mare and her foal, and the *The Curse of Seal Valley*, about the evil of gossip, which is always rife and is often misinformed. Wildfire gossip, embroidered by idle tongues, who make capital out of anything; who twist facts beyond recognition. Always very cleverly, it is based on a grain of truth, so that when you come to listen, you find the kernel of the matter and see how one small incident has been magnified and distorted to make a meal for those with nothing better to occupy their minds.

I thanked Heaven for my old boss. Is it true? Did you check? Well, check again; and for my background of journalistic training, where every fact has to be checked and counter-checked and you have to watch and make sure you don't make mistakes based on mis-understanding. It's easy to, especially with dogs, where you can be talking about four different branches of the same field; those who breed don't always do Obedience; those who do Obedience don't always do Working Trials; those who have pets are not concerned with any of the above. All think differently – training to all four groups just does not mean the same thing.

If I talk about a 'sendaway' to Obedience people, I mean a short run out to a box in a ring, rarely more than twenty-five yards long. If I say 'sendaway' to a Working Trials enthusiast, I mean a run-out of a hundred yards to nothing at all, and then a re-direct of fifty yards to right or left, according to the judge's direction.

When I say 'controlling a dog,' I don't necessarily mean what a breeder means. If I talk about training a dog, a breeder will at once think of the show ring, of standing for the judge and moving for the judge; whereas I don't consider that is training, it is only part of it. I want a dog that stays on command and heels quietly beside me, behaving when I am out.

So much depends on your viewpoint; and when there are so many, there are no rights and no wrongs, only differences, depending on the way you, personally, have chosen to live, or are maybe forced to live.

Chapter Eleven

One of the things one learns as a writer is to keep a diary; to make notes and to keep letters. Everything may come in useful, and letters will prove points made long ago, that other people might think untrue. I knew before I bought her that I would write a book about my new puppy. What kind of book remained to be seen, though I never visualised it would be *this* book. I had quite different plans, with experience behind me. One needs humility and one thing a dog like Chita ensures is that you never make the mistake of glibly dismissing a newcomer to the club. You take the dog and find out just what the owner is up against. Sometimes the owner is to blame; a man may be too hard on a gentle dog: a woman too soft with a tough one. Or someone may be amused by misbehaviour, and not realise this will make the dog act up, playing for laughs. But with so much overbreeding in every breed, temperament is suffering, and what is coming out is so near wild dogs that many people fail to realise they don't have to *train* their dog, they have to *tame* it; and that is a very different matter as you can't start training until you have finished taming.

I made notes on everything I did with Chita and kept a diary in one of Charlie Wyant's Obedience record books, which has been an enormous help to me; I can look back, when I feel depressed, and see how far we have come.

I am going to list it, hoping those with dogs like mine will take note, as it shows just what had to be done to get anywhere near living decently with this little villain. The first page of the diary reads:

Born August 21st, 1977. Nine in the litter.

Came home October 3rd; Inoculated October 3rd and October 31st.

Taken out in car daily, 'walked' in my arms, but not allowed to mix with any dogs but Janus and Puma till after inoculations. Taken to friends who have no dogs and taken indoors to meet them. Very difficult puppy. Easy to housetrain and intelligent. Hated older dogs and excessively noisy.

Socialisation continuous, at saturation point for 18 months. I further noted that she was a very excitable hyper-active pup. Some of that was due to worms, which she had in quantity when I got her. My notes continue; mostly training notes. Chita was then eighteen months old.

Totally steady to gunshot, behind and beside her.

Tracking is coming and now indicates article.

She creeps on downstay and anticipates every exercise.

Control needs to be worked on.

By then, Chita was fine so long as we only met nice dogs; if another dog swore at her, she flew back at him or her, as the rule that dogs don't attack bitches and bitches don't attack dogs doesn't exist in the dog's mind; only in a few books and they are wrong. If a dog feels stroppy he will attack dog or bitch, and there are a few bitches who hate all other bitches and they are a real headache to own; there are also dogs that guard even the daisies and have never been stopped, or they have owners secretly rather proud of being owned by such a loving dog that it allows no one else near them. Everyone else loathes it.

They make it very hard for anyone who does have a timid or a formerly aggressive dog, as it takes years to cure them and only moments to undo all the owner's hard work; I tend to go to shows very warily these days.

Our first relaxation was at Cheltenham; we didn't shine in any way at all, but the evening before the Show I helped put up the rings. Other dogs ran riot but I kept Chita in the car, knowing it only needed one odd word said and she might flip. Also, dogs that race to exhaustion the night before a show, tend to be very tired next day. I want my dogs fresh.

The Show was held at the racecourse, where the dogs were photographed during the day, very successfully, and where for once there were seats so that you could relax by the rings and watch in comfort.

Since Chita needed the socialising most, she was with me almost all day; the older dogs had both retired from competing now and preferred to be in the car, so I sat by the ring, Chita at my feet, and watched everyone work, in the hope of learning by watching.

One day Chita might start to collect rosettes as Janus did; that day was a long way off. If she did her stays, lost only a few points and didn't charge out of the ring or do something insane, which she is quite capable of doing, I would be happy.

It was a lovely sunny day, a rarely sunny day for the summer of 1979, and it wasn't until lunch time that it dawned on me that I was sitting amongst all kinds of dogs: a big German Shepherd was lying beside us, dogs were walking past us, dogs were coming straight towards us and Chita was lying there like a normal dog; no problems, no fusses, no attempt to fly out and snarl.

It was utter bliss.

I didn't care in the least that her performance left much to be desired. John Seal, who had judged at Cruft's, was judging beginners that day and he set a sensible round; no halts except at the beginning and the end. The dog could walk out and really do proper heelwork. When judges introduce three sits in a row, half the dogs lag, waiting for another sit; it isn't a good round or a sensible one at all.

Her stays were by no means good at this stage, as Chita hates being still. This was only her second show as a working dog; the others she had come to and sat out while Janus worked but Janus is almost nine and is getting slow, and it's no fun for me to feel I am pushing an elderly dog round the ring.

With Chita, we were back to learning one another.

She lost $3\frac{1}{2}$ marks in heel-on-the-lead; mostly for wides and major inattention, which was due to her amazement at finding two rings side by side, and another handler and dog walking alongside us with someone commanding it who wasn't commanding her. She seemed baffled by this procedure and was watching first her steward and then the steward in the other ring, which didn't help me at all to get her concentration. It takes time to give dogs show experience. Few young dogs work at all well at their first few shows. Also, few shows have enough space to separate rings properly. Some shows penalise the young dogs from the start, by placing the ring near the entrance or the car park and providing major distractions.

I made a mental note that I needed to work on concentration. Trips to big car parks and try her out there, watching me all the time.

Friends with pups younger than her were already making progress. They were kind, in a rather unkind way!

Heel-Free produced a piece of nonsense which was entirely my fault, as I was wearing a brooch that proved to have a faulty pin. Chita loves catching things and her reactions are very fast. The brooch came unfastened and fell off, and I watched it drop towards her mouth, pin open. I watched her lift her head, ready to catch, so I flipped the lead and brought her past it and as she turned to snatch it from the ground, then stopped and picked it up, which of course lost me a number of marks. We lost 6 marks there. When I called her to me, she came at the beginning of the sentence 'call your dog'. She knew that one, and more work was needed there. John said I should have walked on and ignored the brooch. Unfortunately, Chita didn't intend to ignore it. She knew it should be on me!

She anticipated again on her retrieve and lost $3\frac{1}{2}$ marks but, as she had been very difficult to teach the retrieve to, and wasn't always happy about doing it in public, I was happy enough there. I could work on anticipation; she picked the dumb-bell up, came in fast and held it well.

Stays proved a slight problem as they were on tarmac, and I knew as soon as we went on to it that the ground was hot; and Chita has tender paws. She was being treated for mild eczema. She also proved to have tender other parts, as we faced our dogs and she wasn't sitting right down. However, I think only I was aware that she was a fraction off the ground. She has a very close coat. I had felt the stay area with my hand; it could have been uncomfortable. She stood just *after* the judge had said 'exercise finished' so she didn't lose marks on that, but would have to learn not to move until I told her or she might, another time, move too soon.

The downstay was going to prove a hazard, as I wasn't able to place her where I wanted, which was near to a spaniel and a golden retriever; she had to lie between two black and white collies remarkably like the dog that bit her; she has never liked collies since, though she now endures them.

There were sixty dogs and they were lying close. The collies were good and were still, all the dogs were settled, when suddenly a dog right at the end of the ring saw a friend outside and, just as the competitors had left their dogs and turned to face them, he shot across the ring past all the other dogs and vanished, followed by his owner.

No other dog moved.

Not even Chita, but the dog had suddenly flashed past her nose and she was worried; after about a minute and a half, she began to creep towards me, obviously insecure. She lost 3 marks.

Shows sometimes produce odd hazards. At her first show that year, her dumb-bell had broken as I threw it; we were working on a car park and the ground was gritty and hard. Chita brought in half her bell, after a considerable pause to puzzle out what a dog was supposed to do, faced with two pieces. I didn't want to stop her bringing *something* in – that could have put her off retrieving again in the ring. The judge suggested we borrow a dumb-bell. I wanted to get a spare from my car but there wasn't time.

She didn't like a dumb-bell that smelled of another dog. In fact, my three each have their own bell and I don't let them bring in the others! Scent in the mouth for dogs that have a strong sense of smell must be overpowering. I don't like the taste of soap on my dentist's hands and I only have human taste buds; dogs have very sensitive noses and mouths indeed.

Our next show was near Worthing, where in Beginner she did a very good round indeed, losing only 1¾ marks, for a slight lag and marginally crooked sits. She earned a diploma there; it was her first show at Findon, and Janus had earned a diploma on his last, for 99¼%, so it was a nice beginning.

The novice round was the first I had entered her for, as competition is much harder in that class, where all those who have won even as far as Cruft's, but lost their old dogs, are now back with new ones.

I found a new hazard.

I had socialised Chita so well she adored people. The judge stroked her. 'Stroke . . . in the ring . . . cor, I like that,' said Chita's tail, and she licked the stroking hand.

'I like *you*,' the judge said, smiling at her.

That was a big mistake, as I found I didn't have the least idea what to do with a dog that, every time she passed the judge, turned her body and waved her tail wildly, every inch of her saying, "Cor, I like you too." We lost a cricket score of marks.

But she got full marks for temperament (my awful little savage), and also full marks for her stays, so who cared; the judge fell for her in a big way, and she fell for him and we ended up in laughter. He thought maybe she would work better with a woman judge! Maybe she'd fallen for his sex appeal.

It was obvious that before I could even attempt Working Trials, she would have to be far more under control, as that is what trials are about; and a lot of judges are commenting in their reports on the lower stakes in trials that dogs lacked control.

I saw no point in entering them until I could make a fair showing, though whether I would under examination in a strange place was something else again. There are no trials near us. So it will be expensive to go.

Chita lost 9½ marks in the Findon novice round, which under the circumstances I didn't think at all bad, though a lot of people who have easy dogs would be horrified. Circumstances alter cases and also alter opinions. No way did I expect very much as yet; I had only just begun with Edith, and maybe it would have been better to wait a year before entering shows with Chita, but my dog shows are a day out and I enjoy them. If one only goes to win, one loses a lot from the event. Also, it means I meet old friends and renew old acquaintances. And I can now talk to people with dogs, even when holding Chita, as she behaves.

Our next show was a long way off, as I had entered Okehampton, Devon. With the dog club to run and no helpers as yet to rely on, who were as interested in keeping our standard up and our club going as I was, I couldn't get away for a holiday at all, so was taking long weekends; in places that were as pleasant as possible, picking shows in lovely country. The Liverpool and Manchester round rarely have gorgeous venues or beautiful places to stay, and it was years since I had been to Devon.

I stayed in a motel, where I promptly met an odd problem. I use my credit card to save carrying much money and, if they won't accept that, I use a cheque which is backed by the credit card. The motel refused to accept cheques!

I spent the weekend carefully balancing a mini budget, as petrol had just doubled in price; there could have been a shortage as there had been at Findon, but I just about managed. If I spent fifty pence on my breakfast, which meant coffee and one slice of toast, and had a snack lunch, I could just afford an evening meal, so long as I did without soup and a sweet and coffee! It was idiotic, as I wasn't hard up, just short of ready cash; and no way would they change their minds and take a cheque. They must have been stung in a big way. I also had to pay in advance for my room, which was minute, just room for me and the dogs, and if I got out of bed in the night, I trod on dogs.

I had accepted the booking on the phone and the room was rated as a suite; it was a suite all of twelve feet long and eight feet wide, just room for a narrow bed. My bedside table went neatly under the washbasin, and the chair was jammed between the foot of the bed and the wall. There was a tiny window and it was very hot; and the bathroom was way down the garden. It was quite the oddest "suite" I had ever seen and quite the smallest room I had ever rented for two nights; and not all that cheap.

The Show was held just outside the town, in a good venue. The shows in the south usually have much better grounds than those in the north, where people often have to make do with venues that would rate a load of complaints from southerners. Someone complained about the length of the grass. At one northern show, all you could see of small dogs was a wave in the grass!

The food was good and mercifully was very cheap, so I decided to stoke up during the day and do without an evening meal. I bought sandwiches and took them back with me. It was a fairly hilarious situation. Even then I misjudged, and I found myself on the way home going from pub to pub in search of pub grub at fifty pence, or I wouldn't have enough money for petrol to get me back.

The beginner round was early in the day. We'd drawn fifth. Chita decided that she wasn't going to concentrate; new places, new smells, new dogs. At one point she flipped, and when another dog showed its teeth at her, did her famous lunge and yell act, which infuriated me as she hadn't done it for ages. It wasn't entirely her fault, but I couldn't risk it starting again. I took her up to the car park to give her ten minutes' training; the kind of voice and the kind of check I need on this little exercise is something most people never do need and something I had never dreamed of with Janus and Puma.

Chita just doesn't feel pain, so you have to be as hard on her as you are on a very insensitive horse before she responds. I was suddenly aware, as she defied me and I was giving her a really good snatch of the chain, that two elderly ladies were sitting in their car glaring at me.

Oh, well, they would have to glare, as it was either that or destruction for Chita. If she reverted to going for other dogs, I couldn't go on; it was far too hair-raising for me and, besides, it hurt my arm and she'd already sprained my thumb once, had caused me to have three stitches in my hand and was downright dangerous when she played the fool.

I finished the round, losing 6. Again she had full marks on her stays and the loss of marks was due to her not attending, and going wide; also not anticipating on retrieve, as she adored the dumb-bell by now, having taken ages to learn how to do it, resisting every move.

The novice judge, as far as I could see, was very severe indeed and the marking was very hard. Chita *didn't* work better under a woman. Having been stroked, she thought the aim of the game was to go and be petted again; the judge hadn't the same sense of humour as our previous judge and obviously thought little of my dog. We ended up with a cricket score of marks against us once more, having lost 7 on heel-free, as Chita veered to the judge every time we passed, which I found extremely annoying.

When you work a dog in the ring, you are not allowed to correct mistakes as you do when training. The mistake is a fault and loses you a mark. Some judges are kind and will allow you to treat the round as a training round, but not at competition. Other judges refuse to allow this so sometimes it is better to withdraw than to let the dog make a lot of mistakes which you can't correct. Of course, if you do train in the ring, you forfeit your entry money as you are no longer competing and no score is marked against you.

On this particular day, she stayed perfectly, which was a bonus.

I was getting tired and put her in the car and went to watch the pre-beginners. I had donated rosettes for Best Labrador, Best Golden Retriever, Best Rare Breed, and Best Cross Breed, as I think it is a great shame that Obedience is now becoming a pastime for collies, Shelties and German Shepherds almost exclusively. All breeds were once bred to work and all *can* work.

Edith works a Red Setter in the top class; Bob, who is new to competition though not to dogs, works his Rough Collie; those he breeds have brains.

I want to see Cruft's with fifty different breeds, not just one or two. It is high time people began to train the dogs they have instead of being brain-washed into thinking they must have a collie for the job. It leads to over-breeding, which in turn leads to undesirable dogs. If they continue, we soon won't have people who know a thing about training other breeds.

The pre-beginner judge was someone I had heard of but never met. She had been the partner of one of the first people in Obedience to go to a lot of trouble for me and teach me how to win rosettes with Janus; she was with me the day he won his first two rosettes, an eighth and a tenth at Carlisle, and she was more pleased with those than her own far better win!

I spoke to the judge who had read my articles on Chita, and had come over to see her.

Just like the bitch she had.

Her bitch proved to have the same breeding. She was much bigger and was gorgeous and quite nutty. She had to be chained indoors or she couldn't be left; and her owner, who had trained dog after dog, who'd trained problem dogs and cured sheep stealers, said she went to club with a large black German Shepherd bitch walking on her hind legs, refusing to be controlled, and with a built-in desire to create total chaos wherever she went.

That very dominant grandfather again. I wondered what dogs were like who had him in both parents' ancestry.

I went home much happier, having met someone who had a great deal more experience than I. If she found a dog from that breeding a problem, with all her knowledge and with her profession being dogs, then I wasn't doing too badly with mine.

I hadn't got that far, but time was on my side and there was a goal to aim for.

I sometimes think it must be rather sad to win Cruft's; there is nowhere left to go. No further goal to reach. No great occasion to plan for, no dream to fulfil. Perhaps with another dog – but you may have a young dog and not wish to start a new puppy.

There's an old proverb that says it is better to travel

hopefully than to arrive, and it applies to most things we do. Easy success doesn't bring half the exultation that you have when you watch a small villain change and come under control; when you see the work you have put in begin to pay off; when the hours of despair change occasionally to a light-headed feeling of total ecstasy, as the little monster you thought a maniac runs to her scale. She leaps it, and goes down, waiting patiently for another command, or comes to me and sits with her paws on my knee, telling me (as the others don't) that, please, she needs to go out.

Puma and Janus grunt and go to the door.

Chita tries to tell me, desperate to communicate, using her body as a vehicle for language, and slowly we understand one another.

She sees me pick up her dumb-bell and is all attention. "Now, can I do it now? Are we going to *work*?"

That triggers off Janus too, but it has never triggered off Puma.

It was at this point that work seemed to get on top of me. I was writing both a fiction and a non-fiction book, as well as articles; and the dog club also suddenly grew and there was far too much to do, so that Chita's training suffered. There was never enough time.

Time . . . I chased it, wishing I lived nearer the shops, wishing that I had more help with the club, wishing I had time to get off to get away, as I wanted to go to Perth but couldn't; it was too far. I wanted to visit my aunts, both now in a nursing home, but it was too far. I wished I could go down to Devon again, as the other bitch's owner had given me clues as to what to do with Chita; it was too far.

And of course once I eased up on training, Chita reverted and our next shows were disasters; I might as well not have gone. I never mind not winning, but when the dog goes backwards and even breaks its stays, then defeat sets in and, with loss of confidence, training suffers further, as one gets irritated and has to stop.

Stupid pup; what is she doing wrong and why? What am *I* doing wrong?

So far as I knew, nothing.

Over to Edith to tell her my tale of woe.

"Give her to me," said Edith, looking at me. I was tired, and this pup was a major pain in the neck again just as I thought I was winning.

I sat watching Edith do battle.

Suddenly the penny dropped. *Edith* was having to work almost as hard as I did on this bitch, with all her experience. She *was* winning but she was exerting all her strength on Chita, and she was exerting all her authority on her and she wasn't having an easy ride at all.

It wasn't me. It *really* wasn't me. I'd only half believed that. Partly, yes, it would have to be, but only in small part.

Another show and a judge who was scornful. This time my daughter came with us. Chita adored Anne and didn't see why we should be separated. Work on it, the novice judge said, watching my dog make every mistake in the book and a few not in any book. But since we only see Anne for about five days a year, that was remarkably difficult advice; and anyway I don't mind my dog loving my daughter; I'd be worried if she didn't.

Chita tried to go to Anne on recall and tried to go to Anne in her stays. Not finding Anne, she came to me. She can't bear the family to be separated and pulls like mad if she is leashed and Kenneth walks ahead.

The beginner judge looked surprised when I went over and said I would like to scratch, as my daughter was with me and her presence was causing us problems.

"You paid," he said. "This isn't an ordeal; it's a day out. Work her on the lead and train her; it will be good for her. Keep her on lead in the stays."

I did and it worked and she did pay attention, loving every minute; maybe too I relaxed as I wasn't being marked. It was fun.

I thanked the judge.

"I've got a dog just like her," he said. "That's why I'm

judging. Why don't you judge? She'll have turned you into a far nicer person if you don't let her make you bitter."

It was quite a thought. Unfortunately, under the new rules, I am no longer qualified to judge others. I was before. You can't win!

Our next show managed to make me wonder if one ever could win under anyone. The first round proved disastrous as the rings were very close and a man in the ring next door threw his dumb-bell towards us as we came up to the rope on Heel-Free. Chita saw the dumb-bell and I watched her body tense. She'd go for it; lose points, muck up the round for the man in the next ring and, if she and the dog that owned the dumb-bell met head on, there might be a fight. I could think of only one thing to do, and I did it.

"Don't you dare," I said, in the only voice that Chita understands when her mind is on other things.

I had already lost a cricket score for not doing my turns exactly the way Charlie Wyant taught us to; Edith teaches different types of turn. I can't see that it matters *how* you turn so long as handler and dog are both accurate. I now lost more marks for using a harsh voice on my dog.

Oh, well, at least we hadn't had a confrontation; the judge didn't know my dog. I did.

The next round I decided to play it the "right" way and not use a hard voice on my dog; try cooing to her and handling her as if she were Puma. As we went into the ring, a young dog bit her on the nose which hardly helped, but to my pleasure she didn't even snarl; she looked at me and walked on, a bead of blood on either side of her muzzle.

It wasn't a good round, for Chita *can't* be handled as if she were a dear little sweet dog, and the judge said so, loud and clear. She was one who *did* know her dogs! I needed to handle the bitch differently. She wouldn't have pretty-pretty handling in her ring; Chita needed much more firmness.

I bit back several retorts and a desire to scream, and

went off to make notes on both judges in case I should ever meet them again. I should remember to reverse my methods in their rings or I wouldn't win. I wonder if in fact there is anything in the regulations that lays down the law on how you talk to your dog; surely the need is to have it under control, come what may, not to be sweet with a villain and hard on a soft dog and vice versa?

I decided to give up shows.

This was easier said than done, as I found I could get to Liverpool and to Runcorn in one day, and went to both, obviously being a glutton for punishment. At Liverpool, for some reason known only to Chita, she didn't stay for either the sitstay or the downstay but followed me into the centre of the ring. Our last show had been among remarkably unsteady dogs; some had gone down, some had moved behind her, some had gone into the centre of the ring to their handlers; had she watched and been perverted? I didn't know; all I knew was that she lost thirty points for her stays in both classes; she behaved as if untrained and I had almost given up hope. Thinking it over when we got back, I realised we had had a passenger in the car with his two collies and my dogs were unsettled by strangers in the car.

So, no more passengers, except one who only comes along without a dog and never puts a foot wrong among dogs.

A few other dog owners can come too, though it is not easy if they have to bring a dog. We don't let the dogs mix even on my field. One young spaniel leaped from a car two weeks ago and raced after Chita, who was free on the field as it was her own home.

Chita fled up the field, her ruff bristling, ears flat, that wild look back in her eyes, while the spaniel belted on at top speed. She is intended for gunwork, so no one was pleased at the way she came through a car window we thought too nearly shut to let her out.

"Chita, *down*."

I yelled at the top of my voice. Had my training paid off?

It had.

Chita went down as if I had shot her and lay still, panting in terror. The spaniel looked at her in amazement, heard her owner call, trotted back and was put back in the car.

Chita came to me. No fight; no confrontation; no worry. Maybe she can't win at shows, maybe I never will manage those Working Trial qualifications but at least she can learn and she can obey even when she is terrified.

It gave me hope.

I always need hope with Chita.

We were due to go to Runcorn Show. This was held in a sports centre, and, to my horror, I had been drawn to work second in the ring in the Beginner round. As I had already drawn fifth, drawn third, and drawn first in Novice, at other shows, I wasn't too pleased; Chita is so full of life after a long journey that it is like trying to control an atom bomb with its warhead ready primed and I had never found a way to defuse her.

We were due to work at about 11.00am.

I rang the night before to ask the way.

"Come off the motorway at exit 12 and you will find signs to the dog show."

I did; and I didn't.

No signs.

Almost to Warrington and ask the way.

I should have been told to come off at exit 11.

The other side of the town.

I found the sports centre after some time, and a good deal of asking.

It was the wrong sports centre.

Time was racing by and I was working almost at once; if I lost my place, I couldn't work at all, and I had left home at seven to get here in loads of time.

I asked the way.

I found the sports centre.

It was the wrong sports centre again. Runcorn appeared to have dozens of the things.

I asked the way from a man reading a paper.

"You'll never find it," he said, which was a lot of help.

He must have seen my expression. "Hang on, I'll drive you there, is all I meant," and off he set, me following, and drove around four miles to land me at the sports centre, which was in the middle of nowhere, but only just off the motorway if you'd taken the right exit. Show secretaries, please note!

I raced to the Secretary, miles away from the car park which appeared to be on top of a man-made mountain. I was high above the ground. I collected my number.

The rings were miles away; Chita and I both were in need of a loo, but there wasn't time as it was five past eleven. Wasn't even worth coming. She'd be impossible and I had my mind on other things – though the toilet block was right across the rugby pitch in the opposite direction.

I reached the ring, Chita trotting beside me, all eagerness and verve.

"I'm working second," I said to the judge.

"You're working first," he said. "Number one hasn't turned up. In you go."

I no longer cared. Our scores at Liverpool had been utterly disgraceful. Chita had barely been under control and I had come off the field wishing I had never seen the stupid dog. All that training and she still behaved like a maniac in the ring. She broke both sets of stays, and lost 10 on retrieve for anticipation and playing with her dumb-bell, she had lost on both heel-on-lead and Heel-Free, and I had kept her score a dark secret as with Janus I was ashamed if I lost three marks.

At Liverpool her score was 60 in Beginners, though I have never before or since seen marking like that day; I lost marks for things I had never dreamed of and nor had anyone else.

By the time we got to the novice round I was disgusted with the day, with the judging, with myself and with my dog; we did no better and lost 45, as again she lost 30 on her stays. She anticipated every exercise.

So what did it matter what we did at Runcorn?

I'd retire her after this show and take up tatting; or judging, as I can't make more of a hash of it than one or two people who have judged me in the past.

Or just shoot her and get a dog. She wasn't a dog. She was a disaster. It took all the fun out that, when I trained daily, people thought I had never laid a finger on her.

I put down her dumb-bell on the table and went in. She'd break her stays any way and do an atrocious round. And we would lose 60 again and I hated Obedience. I never minded not winning but I did mind working and working and working on the little fiend, then finding out that whatever else I could trust her to do, I could trust her to both let me down and show me up.

"Joyce Stranger can't train a dog at all."

"OK, try my dog, that's all. Just try the so-and-so. You can have her."

Into the ring and round the ring, Heel-on-Lead. Small dog paying attention . . . *paying attention!* Her otter tail going, looking up at me at every sit. I didn't believe it.

I couldn't believe it.

She couldn't be working at last, could she?

Heel-on-Lead. I lost half a mark for a crooked sit.

On the last time out she'd lost 10 marks for a round that might have been done by one of the new dogs at my club, untrained, untaught, impossible. How many hours had I worked? I didn't know.

Round the ring for Heel-Free and this was where the crunch would come, as there was a ring beside us and another dog working and she hated that. If only she didn't lunge and bark, ruff on end . . .

Although we were working first, a dog had fouled the ring beforehand, a cardinal sin. They had cleared up, but there was slime on the ground; my foot slipped and, as I came to the turn, I knocked Chita's head with my knee. My fault, not hers.

We lost one mark – compared with 10 at Liverpool. And half of that mark was due to me, not to Chita.

If only she didn't anticipate me on the recall.

I went out, leaving her.

"Chita – *wait!*"

I kept my hand behind me which is allowed, in the wait position. I kept it out in front of me when I arrived and turned, still in the wait position and said 'wait' again for good measure.

"Call your dog."

I left my hand stopping her from coming, said "Chita, come," and moved my hands swiftly to the right position. She flew in, sat in front and waited until the steward said 'finish'. I counted five and sent her round, hoping by that to stop her flying round at the next show as she learns some things too well.

Half a mark gone for a crooked sit at the end, as she was so eager to do right that she sat to look into my face.

Am I a good girl?

I was feeling light-headed.

Now for the retrieve which she adores, and can't wait to get to the dumb-bell. At one show she rushed after it and tried to catch it before it fell. I had to make her wait.

"Chita – wait!"

"Throw your bell."

I threw, trying to get it dead straight, which is never easy. She'd have to come in at an angle.

"Chita – wait!"

"Send your dog" . . . and she went on "dog", before I could stop her.

Off to fetch the bell, a lovely pick-up and dead straight in. Dead straight on the finish, as perfect as could be except for 2 marks lost for anticipation. If she hadn't gone, she'd have had full marks – which is the story of most people's show lives.

We lost 4 marks. We weren't in the first six even if she did her stays which was most unlikely, having broken at two shows. She'd not stayed for one second but followed me in to the middle. I remembered too that just before she'd gone into the ring at Porth Madoc, she had been bitten on the nose. "Can't stop dogs doing that, can you?" said an owner I'd have liked to throttle, having spent a year or more doing just that with my own demon bitch.

So maybe that was why she broke; didn't want to be bitten again and who would blame her, as she'd had a very bad bite at an impressionable age and that hadn't helped at all. It could have accounted for all her problems.

We worked her Novice round before the Beginner stays.

It was a stiff round; she lost 2 in Heel-on-Lead, 3 in Heel-Free, her recall was full marks and her retrieve I managed to prevent any anticipation from, and she only lost half a mark on that; a big improvement. She sat crooked at the end again looking at me, "Was I good?"

Pup, you were angelic, blow the heel marks; that was a big change.

Our downfall was left turns of which there were a good few, and lags, which I knew were due to the numerous rounds we had done, constantly interrupted by halts; these make dogs that are bright anticipate another halt and slow down for it, and look as if they are lagging.

I had been told by a very experienced judge to scratch any round in future that included a lot of halts, as it's bad for heelwork and bad judging. Only when one has paid and driven a long way, one wants to enter.

Stays.

The dogs were lined up. I could place her where I liked. She had been bitten by one German Shepherd, chased by another, bitten by a collie and both proliferate in Obedience these days.

In the corner, between a spaniel and a cross-bred that didn't look at all like a collie:

"Leave your dogs."

We could face them. I had placed Chita carefully; no thistles, nothing on the ground to tempt her, a fair way from the other two dogs, with her back to the middle rope and no one likely to walk behind her or stand behind her with another dog.

"Stay, Chita, stay," I was willing her with all my mind through the longest minute I remember.

"Return to your dogs."

She hadn't moved. I looked above her head, stood beside her, careful not to touch her.

"Exercise finished."

I didn't praise her then, but heeled her two steps, lead on, and made an enormous fuss. " Clever girl. Lovely girl. You are clever."

If only she did the down . . .

"Chita – down – *stay*."

I heeled her across the ring and back, and settled her. The grass was long and might tempt her, and if she began to sniff or chew she would move.

"Leave your dogs."

This time a two-minute agony. I watched her, trying not to catch her eye. A quarter of a minute. She hadn't moved. Half a minute; another dog had moved. Three quarters of the minute and two more dogs had moved, but not Chita.

If only she would stay. Stay, I willed, stay, hoping she was telepathic. I would never be able to endure ten minutes out of sight.

One minute.

Another bitch moved and the bitch next to Chita turned on one hip. She turned her head to look at her.

"Stay," I willed, not daring to breathe, repeating the word in my brain.

One and a quarter minutes and the next-door bitch got up and came to its owner.

I couldn't concentrate harder if I tried. My face ached with keeping still and willing my dog to stay. "Chita, stay." Inside my head, over and over.

One and a half minutes.

The bitch on the other side of her was looking round for its owner. Another bitch got up. Someone ran past the ring with a dog on the lead, bouncing merrily.

One and three quarter minutes.

"Return to your dogs."

She hadn't moved; she *must* stay down now. I didn't touch her, didn't look at her, and when again the Steward said "Exercise finished," I clipped on her lead, heeled her out of the ring and hugged her, telling her over and over how clever she was.

She sat gazing into my eyes, trying hard to understand this fool woman who set such store on her keeping her still like that in a ring with other dogs when I knew she hated other dogs, feared other dogs, had been bitten and chased by other dogs.

I hoped we weren't going to go through our show life adding to the list of dogs Chita had been bitten or chased by till there were no breeds left she liked.

I remembered Puma sitting trembling in the ring at a show, not moving an inch, with twenty collies and after a bad bite from a collie tied under a table. I didn't see the dog; it leaped out and bit. At the next show, Puma wouldn't get out of the car unless dragged, and for weeks after she did her stays trembling so much I could see her shaking, and felt a heel.

I looked at our score; that day Chita had come straight out of the car and worked and only lost four marks. She had stayed through two sets of stays.

It was our last show of the season.

All winter to work on her.

And next year, what?

I don't know and nor does she.

I must go and train her; she still hates stays. She adores movement.

I must train the older dogs, or they get out of hand and won't come and are jealous; next year we might be ready for our first Working Trials; we might do better at shows; they have changed the rules so that it is possible to try the higher classes without having to be first out of sixty before you can have a go.

Chita is now much easier to take about. I have a divided dog guard and the two German Shepherds travel together and His Lordship sits regally on his own, having elected to go that side; I left it to the dogs to decide who should travel where.

I open the hatchback.

"Stay."

Chita is learning at last to stay in the car, learning to be more sensible, learning to come with me off-lead close at heel, though never where there are sheep and never where there is traffic and never where there is a danger of other dogs attacking her.

She is too precious for that.

My little villain.

My little horror.

My hope for the future.

No longer a screaming maniac; just a whimper if she needs out or is trapped in a room, though she is sometimes very excited when she wants to get out of the car, but then so is Puma.

They all get excited if we go to the beach; it's a training place and my dogs love being trained. Into the slip chain and sit, ready for off.

"Chita, heel."

"I like doing that." Her eyes glow.

"Chita, come."

"Can't come fast enough."

"Chita, *seeeek*."

And down her head goes and she's off on her trail, little hunter following hidden messages that I shall never understand.

People who don't work with their dogs don't know what they are missing.

People who don't train their dogs don't know what it feels like to have the dog with you, enjoying every moment of its day, longing to be shown yet another exercise, a different exercise, leading either to competition or the bonus of a well-behaved companion.

It never just happens. It's very hard work.

And the rewards are too great to value in any normal terms.

Chapter Twelve

Chita is progressing at last. Yesterday we had a tracking session here. It was a wet day, the rain pouring down. There were to be six of us; with instruction from a serving police officer, a dog handler who had very kindly agreed to come and give us a lesson. I had made two huge panfuls of soup, and we were to have soup, bread and cheese and apples, and then go out and track at Miss Marchel's farm, where I trained Boy a lifetime ago; in the days before Chita.

At 11.00am, my neighbour phoned. 'Had we any power?'

I switched on the light. Nothing happened. No power; and no food as we are all-electric. Also, the heating had just gone off and it wasn't very warm.

The cars arrived, and everyone came at once, soon to be followed by our police-dog handler with his son and daughter. He talked about tracking; about laying tracks, about wind, and about scent, and the trail that the dog followed.

There was still no heat so we went out in convoy down to the farm, where everyone stood in the rain dragging on Wellingtons and heavy-weather gear, things no one who is out with dogs should be without.

I had left the two older dogs at home and only had Chita, who was already "singing", having seen her tracking harness. This was the test of my training. A track would be laid for her to follow; and I would be under scrutiny, this time from an expert. I had more or less taught myself, from John Cree's book and Peter Lewis's book, with brief lessons from my two police-dog handler friends and from Jack Cree. I could ring Jack, but it's not easy to describe a track by phone!

We went out down the lane. The field I had chosen had cattle in and we didn't fancy that. They are curious and

172

would come close, and Chita isn't too fond of animals that tower above her, though she now tolerates them. When a pup, she panicked and danced, trying to slip her collar and bolt.

The second field is our familiar field, where Chita and I spend time together; she knows it well. I had left her in the car and we stood in the rain and listened to the finer details of track-laying and then, as we are not far advanced, I watched while the track was laid. Across to a tree, a sharp right turn, an article laid on the ground for her to find, and then on to another turn and down the trail to her favourite glove, which is an old sheepskin glove, soft and catchable and smelling of me.

I went back for Chita, and brought her out of the car, harness over my shoulder; I had her lead and slip chain but she needed to be empty before she began to track so I let her run, aware that now she would not now go racing off and would come as soon as I called. There were strangers there to distract, so I had biscuits in my pocket; she always comes for food.

She did all a dog should and I whistled her in and she trotted slightly ahead of me, turning often to look at her harness. If dogs don't empty before tracking they will often empty on the track. Practising, it loses concentration, showing, it loses marks and may cost you a qualifier.

"Am I going to track?"

She waited by the gate. Often I start the track just inside the gate, but today it began halfway across the fields, so into her ordinary neck chain, lead on, and over to the pole that marked the start of her trail.

She leaped into her harness, head in so fast that she got a leg in the wrong place and had to wait, bursting to begin, while I got it right. The harness was wet and so were my hands and I was slow and clumsy. She whined with impatience "Get a move on, do!"

She knew there was a track; she had actually tracked the trail layer across the field to the pole.

Harness on at last, I checked the line to make sure there

173

were no tangles. There's nothing worse than a dog running free, hot on the scent with a line that won't run out and pulls the dog off the track. Nothing must disturb concentration and, for the dog, it is intense concentration.

Down went Chita's nose. I stood quite still, letting her cast on her line, making sure I didn't move, a cardinal sin.

Off she went.

Chita tracking is pure delight. Her small body is intent, every muscle seemingly tensed, her head is down, 'reading' the ground, thinking over the messages she is receiving. Her tail moves slowly from side to side, as if also helping her as she works. She is total concentration, breathing deeply and evenly and, as she becomes sure of the scent, she runs out to the end of the line and we are moving.

Stand over the article, pick it up and give it to me. She knew that one and we were right, and with a command she didn't really need she was off again. At one pole she was distracted; we had never tracked in rain before and the lovely long green grass was wet; she tried to eat and I stopped her.

"Chita, no. Seeeeek."

She cast again and I stood, trying not to foul her up. When she is tracking I am totally in her hands; I have no idea what she finds there on the ground, how she uses her nose, or what scent she is getting. Some from my shoes; some perhaps from shed hairs and shed skin which they say happens all the time we move; scent from bruised earth and scent from bruised grass, and scent from the crushed wild flowers and insects that die when we tread so carelessly over the ground.

There are other scents too; of rabbit droppings and pheasants that lurk in the fields here, and partridges too, but she ignores those scents. She is working out a line, and my training is paying off as again she has the trail and her head goes down and her tail weaves and off she goes, a small determined mass of muscle, fit as a dog can be, enjoying something only a trained dog can enjoy. The feeling of total pleasure and excitement that comes from following her is impossible to describe.

I thought briefly of taking her to be civilised, centuries ago. I never thought that day could lead to this. I'd no hope then of achieving anything. Had I not tackled this little oddity myself, and let others teach her for me, I would have missed more than I could ever describe, even to those who have trained an easy dog to track.

We were running now and she had the scent of the glove in the air and was on to it, and I tossed it as I took off her harness and she rioted briefly, joyously. "Aren't I clever? Aren't you pleased? Aren't I good?" That toss and throw, and exultant run-out and return to my hand tells her all she needs to know, and she comes back to be leashed and stand moderately quietly as we discuss the track.

A good track and she's doing well and we can now progress to tracks laid when I am not there; to unseen tracks, to prepare for those trials next year; a goal to aim at, a place to go.

I have found all my life that to enjoy living at all, I must have goals. Not goals that the family achieve, although those are also wonderful when they come, but achievements of my own. Another book to write and finish; a permanent state of trying to lose ten pounds; I lose the same ten pounds over and over (some people never learn some things).

Life with Chita now is all plans; out in the morning and over the jumps, to get control at the end of the jump

"Chita, down. Stay down."

She is beginning to, even though she is so full of life that the downstay is an agony, a position to hold with a major effort, not one in which she relaxes. Janus and Puma on downstay settle down and will go to sleep, forgetting they are 'on duty'. Not Chita. She lies tense and alert, her eyes on me, never moving from my face, her body coiled ready to spring and I have to hold her down by will power as I return, or she is up, eager and ready to run. I don't want that as it is the point at which trouble begins at big shows, when owners who don't know any better relax their dogs and the wild excitement of doing something right takes over and they go 'high' and turn on one another and fight. I have seen it happen time and again and most people don't know why.

Their training is at fault.

A calming exercise must end calmly or there is no point in training it at all. A dog that is staying must stay until told to move and then move gently, not be released from tension as a catapult is released from a sling.

I had to re-think everything I did with Chita. I had to think about the way I taught her. She was very fast, she reacted swiftly; she learned an exercise so well she knew it as well as I did and, trying to please me, did it in such a way that she would lose points at shows. She knew the ropes and she knew the routine. I had to think always about not exciting her.

Never overpraise; never move too fast.

I have never had to socialise a dog so much. Without that socialisation she would have remained a lunatic. She had to meet people; she had to meet dogs.

I had never any real choice, as life to me is something you never give up on, and you don't give up with a dog while there is a chance that you can change the animal into something fit to live with. She had endeared herself to both of us; even Kenneth now found her amusing; she was always so wildly wrong!

He had peace while I socialised her. He went boating while I went off to the far ends of the country; maybe Devon, maybe Scotland. Now he has sold his boat and is land-bound – which will make a difference to the way we all live. I've felt guilty going to those shows, but we've worked so hard together I would like to see how we fare, just for a couple of years.

Chita in two years has travelled over thirty-thousand miles; she must have met around three thousand dogs one way and another; and she has added immeasurably to my own knowledge. She will continue to add, as she is unpredictable.

She may in the end be like my neighbour's dog. Telling

me of a bitch he once had, many years ago, a bitch sounding remarkably like Chita, he said, "There was one thing I could always rely on Meg to do. Let me down."

We are at a transition stage; this winter we train with trials in mind; with some Obedience in mind; with control always in mind. Maybe we will get there, maybe we won't. But whatever the outcome, I have learned so much more, as although two's company, there's no doubt that three's a pack. And that is a thing very different, requiring quite different management.

Chapter Thirteen

It is never easy to judge one's own dog. There is always bias, however hard you try. You live with the animal and it needs to be a very unpleasant animal indeed that doesn't entwine its way into your affections.

The past influences one. Chita hadn't been entirely my own choice, which could have affected me too, without me even realising it. It is easy to accept that the dog you picked out very carefully with immense care and research may be a disappointment, as there isn't a person in the world who can possibly guarantee that any form of animal will turn out as intended.

But when you have been made to change your mind . . . that can be different.

I decided, therefore, to include with this book letters from people who know me and who know Chita, and who have no reason whatever to show bias. In fact, they could well not have told the truth about her; but I stressed that I wanted a totally honest opinion with no care taken of my feelings in the matter, and I would print the letters exactly as written.

My first letter was from Jean Graves. I had met Jean and Ian three years before when I first came to live here. I went over for dog food, found an enormously friendly place, full of dogs; kennels that are extremely well run and which I recommend and use myself; and the kind of conversation I was starving for. About dogs. Not dog owners, not show dogs, not dog breeders; about dogs.

I go over about once a month now, and always stay longer than I originally intended, looking at pups, admiring the latest born, though they aren't always what Jean and Ian wish; they sell the ones that don't come out right at a lower price than the others. They had three recent disappointments; nothing wrong with the dogs and lovely healthy pups, but not the shape or colour they were hoping to breed on.

I knew I could trust Jean's opinion as she is very dog wise, and herself has had considerable experience in re-training dogs with suspect temperaments. She has had at least two that her husband did not want to keep; they now come to greet me quietly as I come through the gate. One of them is a huge bitch, nearly shoulder high. She must have been a real handful when she didn't behave. It was partly Jean who kept me working on Chita.

The other thing I like about Jean and Ian is that they won't breed from any animal with a suspect temperament. They are adamant about that; so though Jean turned both these bitches into civilised, sensible animals, a pleasure to be with, neither has ever had pups and never will. Jean wrote:

Dear Joyce,

I was delighted to see the progress that Chita has made since I last saw her three months ago. She worked so well outside the kennels even with all my dogs causing chaos at the gate. She obviously enjoys her Obedience work now, as she works so willingly with eyes on you and tail wagging. That *certainly* is a tremendous difference from the last time I saw her. You have certainly put a lot of hard work into Chita to get over her determined streak. Her temperament has improved and she is a lot more sociable.

Looking forward to seeing Chita track next time you come.

Love,
Jean.

My next letter is from a friend of much longer standing. I went in 1968 to Findon Downs dog club to talk on dog behaviour. They put on a demonstration of dog training for me, and in fact this was the first time I had seen a formal dog club, though I had trained dogs myself, by my own methods, all my life.

I was most intrigued, so that as soon as I bought Janus, two years later, I made sure I started him at our local dog club. Pat O'Shea and Anne Malcolm Bentzen were both members at Findon, Pat with Butch, a dog with a history of his own; and Anne with Bosun, a beautiful Samoyed who died last year; she now has Sailor who is even more beautiful in some ways, though nothing like her first dog.

I saw little of Pat and Anne that year but over the years we have become firm friends. When I go down to Findon for their show I stay in a caravan and help get the rings ready. Visit their home for meals, and take my dogs with me. Last year Chita wasn't welcome and we had major problems; I felt despair when I went. Anne and Pat were tactful; Anne was wary of her new pup, and Pat was equally wary of her old veteran. Janus and Puma have visited for the last few years without the slightest worry. Chita was something different.

Pat's letter came unexpectedly. It fits so well into the book that I am quoting it too. She knows me well enough to be outspoken; so does Anne. Pat wrote:

Dear Joyce,
I have been meaning to write to you for weeks now to say congratulations on the progress you have made with Chita. Looking back at the photograph of our magnificent five, I would not have recognised her for the hell-cat you brought down the previous year!
I dread to think what would have happened if we had turned Chita and Sailor loose in the garden that first year, but this year it was a perfect delight to see them haring up and down with that ridiculous stick. If only I'd got the cine out; the stills don't really show it properly even if the blurred outlines do indicate the speed at which they were travelling!
I know the problems you have faced with Chita and am sure that you have had plenty of "back-seat drivers" advising and criticising your actions. You know the problems I had with Butch (or Grandad as he is now known), but all the worry and hard work is worth it

when your dog can see another dog misbehaving and sit there with a disapproving look on her face!

You had to show Chita who was Boss, just as I did with Butch; and while I know you hated doing it as much as I did, when the only alternative is a one-way trip to the vet, it is amazing how much resolution one can muster, isn't it?

I believe the biggest hurdle to overcome with any problem dog is to identify the cause of the problem. With Butch, his aggression was fear-motivated. Towards people it was specific (ie blonde hair and hats) – I'll bite them before they can belt me – it was easy. I'm still not sure about his aggression towards other dogs. There were no physical signs of his having been bitten by another dog; he may have been over-protective towards me, he certainly had a well developed guarding instinct.

I tend towards the theory that it sprang from basic insecurity – perhaps he had been supplanted by another dog in his first home and thought I might do the same.

Chita had a dominance problem together with her dietary difficulties which added up to a hyperactive temperamental GSD with a large capacity for trouble. The Chita that posed those moments with Sailor could have been a totally different dog.

I think Chita was very lucky indeed to be yours. Her fate otherwise doesn't bear thinking about. How much thought, time and plain hard work would most people have spent on her? As for those people who knew so much better what you should do, I only hope they never find themselves in a similar situation as it would mean another dog needing a new home or ending up in an incinerator. The greatest thrill I get nowadays is seeing my once savage dog sitting next to a nervous or temperamental dog at the club. I think calmness and contentment must seep out of his ears because eventually it calms the nerves of dogs (and, brother, have we had some nervy ones). One day you will experience something like this with Chita, and I hope your critics will have eyes enough to see it!

Pat's writing through this letter got larger and larger and she ended:

I must apologise for my handwriting, but the more strongly I feel about something the larger my handwriting gets.

Yours, in haste,
Pat.

I had written saying I was a bit depressed; I now know Butch well; he is nearly fourteen and a reformed character; but when I first met Pat he was a major headache, a source of considerable stress and of much speculation, as it's always the handler who gets the blame. Pat and I have a very strong fellow feeling as we have both been through exactly the same experiences, including all the well-meaning and quite useless advice from people who don't understand what is involved because they have never in their lives met a dog like that.

What is very plain is that training builds confidence. Chita now knows how I react in circumstances she has met before; my reactions will be absolutely predictable as I have trained myself to react in certain ways and, as a result of knowing what to expect, she watches for that signal, obeys it and calms down at once.

If I had known what I now know when I first had Janus, and had met Edith then, the story of my dogs might have been very different; but we can all be wise by hindsight and, unless we learn from our experiences, they are useless. If we do learn, they are invaluable.

As a result of what I have learned through Chita, I am in a position that very many club trainers are not: I have reshaped a dog with major problems and if one comes to me, and I think it can be changed, then I can try to do so. It may not work. That will depend on the owner's devotion to his or her dog, not on me. I can only advise; I can't take the dog and make it over; if I did, it would be my dog and useless for them.

Again, had I had the experience I have now, Chita would have been less of a problem. But I needed to be trained myself to deal with a dog much harder and much more aggressive to other dogs, and much more dominant than any I had met before. Luckily, they are rare.

The letters about Chita continued to come; every time I have visited anyone this year I have been delighted to add yet another to a collection that has given me hope.

My next letter came from Anne Malcolm Bentzen who, with Pat O'Shea, teaches at Findon.

The part of her letter dealing with Chita reads:

What a pleasure to see you and the dogs this summer. It is always a pleasure to see you with Janus and Puma but after last summer I was rather dreading the arrival of Chita. Instead of the half wild and distinctly schizophrenic dog you brought last year, Chita was a joy to have around. Last year I almost expected her to try and eat my fluffy Sammy puppy, thinking he was a rabbit or something, this year they played as if they were old friends and what a pleasure it was to watch them romping.

Do you remember the evening we spent with Ron Tribe in Worthing? He can do almost anything with any dog, but Chita would not settle at all and he could not get through to her. The wild look was in her eyes the whole evening and she whined and fussed the whole time.

This year she was full of life and energy, but it was playfulness and fun rather than wildness and a distinctly savage potential as before. Please can you let me know something how you have worked this miracle because we get problem dogs in the club, though I'm glad to say we have yet to have one as bad as Chita, and it is difficult to know what to do for the best sometimes.

The last letter I quote comes from Christine Williams, who runs a boarding kennels, so she too has had experience of plenty of dogs. She writes:

Dear Joyce,

It was with great pleasure that I watched Chita tracking on Sunday. A very happy dog in her work, which I would say is very necessary to her. A friend of mine had a nephew of your bitch's, but he was bought as a pet and did no work. They were sensible enough to realise he was going to become impossible as a house dog and sought help. The dog was chasing and circling people when walked off the lead; and even on the lead was a handful. At home he was clearly unhappy, never settling, but prowling round the house. Happily he was able to go for police training, where no doubt he will realise his potential. His owners are now proud owners of a real gentleman; again, a German Shepherd.

Yours sincerely,

(signed) Christine Williams.

Then came the assessment of Edith Collins and Bob Nichols (now Mr and Mrs Nichols). I don't think I could have taken it a year ago; I felt too defeated. But in retrospect, it is totally fair in every way, even if it presents a far from flattering picture of me as I was then! Edith writes:

Our introduction to Chita was so distasteful that Bob and I agreed it was highly likely she would have to be put down. Here was Joyce Stranger, desperately clinging to a lunging, screaming, snappy bitch, which within twenty minutes produced an extremely exhausted handler. Had Joyce done any training with her at all? Was the bitch quite mad? The fire in her eyes certainly led one to believe that she was. No dog apart from her own two mates, Janus and Puma, was safe with her.

We had a quiet word with Joyce, and her feelings towards Chita were, at that time, rather mixed. She had obviously tried very hard to train her and had spent many hours from each hard-working week, in a desperate attempt to socialise her and to teach her some good manners when away from home.

For many years Joyce had longed to have a German

Shepherd she could work in Trials. She was obviously so disappointed in Chita, and yet for all her faults, loved her dearly and no way did she want to give up.

Joyce had entered for the beginners' section of our handlers course, so off she went – being towed by Chita, to Bob's group. Our aim at Carreg Ddu is to teach the handlers to train their own dogs. As it came to Joyce's turn for individual attention, it was quite apparent that she must have extra help with Chita. With all due respect, Joyce is no youngster and, combined with the fact that her hands were riddled with arthritis, there was no way in which she could outwit this determined little bitch, who was gifted with uncanny strength and only lived to prove to the world that she was going to have her own way at all costs. Bob asked Joyce's permission to handle Chita. She must learn her lesson, now or never. As soon as she realised that Bob was getting the better of her, she decided her next move was to sink her teeth into him. That was her undoing. She was not to know that Bob had just completed fifteen years army career, where he had trained men to fight and to take care of themselves under conditions worse than Chita ever dreamed about. His reactions were much faster than any human she had encountered up to now; and so after a nasty argument for a few seconds, Chita decided she had better give this human best, for a while at least. As the weekend progressed, we saw some improvement in Chita, but what pleased us most was that we could see the confidence beginning to build up in Joyce. She proved to us that she knew quite a lot about dogs, and had in fact tried very hard indeed to make this bitch understand what was required of her.

Joyce was the first to admit she still had much to learn, and also understood that Chita must have sound basic obedience before she could ever take her to Trials. It was going to be an uphill struggle and hours of hard work had to be put in each week. Fortunately time was on our side, Chita was only eighteen months old, had plenty of intelligence and was geared to work. She was bounding with tireless energy. Could Joyce stick at it? we wondered.

Throughout that bitterly cold November weekend we watched handler and dog. Control improved immensely. The co-operation of the nineteen other people on that course was fantastic. They all wanted to learn, they all wanted to help wherever possible. We had some superb results and, most of all, Chita was beginning to realise that when other dogs on the course appeared, she must stay quietly by her handler's side. We discovered that Joyce could 'stick at it.' The weather did not deter her, and at the end of the weekend we knew that she was sincere. She desperately wanted to train Chita – and she *was* prepared to work, but needed more help. Her handler faults were many, but when criticised constructively there was no resentment. She listened and she made notes – determined to make progress. She asked us if she could telephone us for advice. We were not entirely happy about this, as Chita could make so many false moves to outwit her handler we decided it would be better if we could watch this little fiend for ourselves. We invited Joyce to come over to us once a week so that we could work on a prepared syllabus and be able to see progress or otherwise, and this arrangement was agreed. We worked on one lesson a week with Joyce and Chita religiously doing their homework; breaking each exercise down into as many parts as we could to avoid confusion setting in.

Slowly – very slowly – and not without many setbacks, the little bitch began to improve. She was, to say the least, a canine example of Jekyll and Hyde. This had to be stamped out. She *must* become more dependable. We began to wonder how long it would be before we would be able to even think of taking the lead off. As the months went by, all the hard graft and hours of thought which had to be put into preparation for each week's work, began to pay off.

Many people would have given in, but not Joyce. As her confidence grew, so did her determination. So much so that she enrolled on a week's Instructor's course at Carreg Ddu, at the end of which she had to sit a stiff examination to qualify as an instructor. She passed this at Instructor's level and gained 91%.

Following this success, Joyce continued her weekly visits for help with Chita. We continually thought up new distractions which could be used in training. We controlled her play and turned it into part of an exercise, using the long line. She thoroughly enjoyed working now, and it is indeed a pleasure to see her off lead at last. Eleven months ago this was just a wild dream.

Much work still remains to be done with Chita, but then success only comes before toil in dictionaries.

(signed) Edith Collins

Much work still remains to be done; the next instalment isn't lived through yet, though nearly a year more will have passed before this gets into print; and who knows?

I never count chickens; I wrote a book called *Never Count Apples* from a saying of my grandmother's 'Don't count your apples till the fruit is on the tree.' Even though the blossom is set, the wind may still blow them off.

Janus and Puma are in their beds as I write; my little demon is curled up on the chair (trust her). Dogs are allowed on the chair in my study, but it is usually Janus who is there, honoured because of his years. Somehow, they have changed places and she has usurped the favourite sleeping place, on the only chair in the house where dogs are allowed.

She is curled up, nose to tail, sound asleep; unlike the old days when she was alert and edgy, ready to leap up and shriek at the slightest sound. Now she has a framework in which to live and each new lesson learned brings security; a pattern which I try never to vary, as she in particular notices variations and becomes puzzled. "Her hand's in the wrong place; does she mean something different today?" She looks at me, a question in her eyes.

She comes to me, and gazes long and deep into my eyes. John Holmes says never trust a dog that can't return your gaze so, if that is a true criterion, I have found myself quite a dog. She gazes and gazes, leaning on me. "Do you love me? Am I good girl now?" I don't know what is in her brain; but I do know that no other dog I have ever lived with, and I have lost count of the number, has ever trusted me enough to share her bone, and her thoughts. Janus and Puma will let me take their bones away – but share them, no. Their bones are very precious to them.

Chita shares her bone and Chita brings me her finds in the fields. Chita will work endlessly, tirelessly, always at my side; now doing, to the best of her ability, all that I ask.

She wants to know more, to learn more, and so do I.

Without her, I wouldn't be the person I am today; I might have had an easier dog, an easier haul and an easier ride to the top. I might be sitting now among those who brag that they are among the Greats, having won out of all the classes we have yet to try, but may never win.

That will never be important.

We have come a very long way together in two years. Two years ago I did not expect I would ever be able to relax with her at any show; two years ago I did not expect that I would travel so widely with her, meet so many people through her, learn so much through her.

Two years ago I despaired of ever being able to help her, because it was always plain that her problems did not lie in her but in her ancestry. At times she seemed to be aware of her own defects, and to be unhappy through them. She wanted to co-operate but she didn't know how. Now she knows.

Now we have a well-established routine. We work together, daily. Now her naughtiness is just naughtiness; running off with my glove, an impish glint in her eyes, but bringing it to me the moment I tell her; picking up the quoit, and teasing Janus with it. "Come on, pull." Provided the competition isn't too rough, they pull together, amicably, both enjoying the game. A year ago I would have had to stop it or there would have been trouble.

Provided I remember always to let the older dogs out first, to put the older dogs in the car first, there is never trouble. If Chita goes out first, mysteriously, she defends her territory; if they are out first, the need vanishes. I have never worked out why.

She will try and stop both dogs getting into the car if she is there first, but will stay beside the car, not moving, and let them in and then follow.

She can greet Kenneth happily without puddling at his feet; she can last through the night like a normal dog. We discovered she has a mild form of Janus's pancreas trouble but, since she was put on to tablets for it, she has put on weight and become much calmer. Permanent indigestion can't be much fun, even for a dog, and that was probably part of her trouble. We only found out recently. She has had the treatment for nearly four months now. She no longer has to drink the tap dry daily.

Years of conditioning have meant that neither Kenneth nor I sleep late. Kenneth always had to be out of the house by about 6.45am to catch his bus to work. Now he is retired he still wakes early and goes down to make a cup of tea for us both before we get up. Chita greets him happily; no puddles now. It is weeks since I used to have to go down and mop up.

By 7.15am she is calling me, softly. She does now need to go out; so down I go, dog biscuits handy, and out she goes. She then comes in fast for her early snack, which she eats while the other two vanish briefly up the field.

I work, often from 8.30am to 12.30pm, with a brief break for coffee and for the dogs to run free. Chita comes with me to get the post from our mail box some distance from the house. She carries home one or two letters, her head held proudly, her tail wagging thoughtfully, full of importance as she is a working dog.

If our mole has disfigured the lawn, she hands me the

189

letters and erases all traces, giving a good sniff at the hole she has left just in case he is under it.

The other two dogs go out for a short run, and then all the dogs lie still, while I finish work.

By lunchtime they know the routine. The papers are put away, and I go to make a snack, perhaps for both of us or perhaps only for me, as Kenneth may have different ideas. If he is busy in the garden or making something in the garage, he wants to eat late, and we need to go out.

Lunch is soon over and the dogs are ready, watching me, bringing me gloves and scarf and hat if it is winter, Janus dragging the lead; Chita waiting by the door. Once the door is opened, the older dogs run to the car: Chita waits her turn.

The car is the gateway to pleasure. It may be a walk, or training, or a track. It may be a visit; it may take them anywhere. They never know; though they do know several of our more usual training places and recognise the route, sitting up eagerly when we arrive.

Training Chita is no longer exhausting; it is rewarding and fun for both of us and as a result I am no longer so tired. Also, I have no need now to stay up till midnight if I don't wish, to make sure her nights are short and no accidents happen when Kenneth goes downstairs.

In the past we had begun to wonder if she would ever grow out of the habit.

Now we can both laugh at the dogs; giving Chita her biscuit is no longer liable to end in a finger that is marked because she is too eager. It was never a bite. She didn't mean to do it.

That might have been the motto for all her young life.

She never meant it; she couldn't help it. She wasn't wicked; she was programmed, from the start; programmed by ancestors she will never meet or know about. I have learned about her ancestry now. I know very well that sometimes, not very often, the mixture of dogs of her breed in the past can give pups just like her. We have met several and heard of several more.

I knew when her niece and nephew came for training

that it wasn't me; it wasn't Chita. It was those dogs from long ago, making a working dog; a dog bred to work, a dog that had to work. Her nephew showed himself to be a born police dog; without control he might well have become a killer. He is now a very successful working dog in a Midland police force.

His owner has another dog now. He was bred from pet lines and is a great character; very patient, angelic with her new baby; in class a little self-conscious, a little amused to find himself having to perform for her among other dogs, but tolerant of her desire to work with him. He is very like Puma in his nature, and looks like her father did, a big, noble, beautiful and dignified dog.

Chita, in a few minutes, will be first at the door, and if I don't open it fast, she will open it. The other dogs don't open the house doors. Chita can. She will be first down the passage and into her bed, to wait for our afternoon treat. If the weather is too bad to go out and we are snowed in, she has to be trained up and down the hall and in the sitting room; and the dogs practise long downstays, for ten minutes at a time, to ensure that they do have some occupation.

I am writing this at the beginning of 1980. The world is changing fast. Listening to the news, one wonders if life will go on as it has done for the past forty years; if there will still be petrol to get about; if there will still be dog shows. When Puma first entered Championship shows, I paid £1 at the most for her entry fee. This year it costs £5 a time for each entry at Cruft's. Championship shows are £3.50 each. It cost me £22 for petrol when I went down to Devon.

There may never be the chance to show what she can do; it will be sad, if so, as it would be fun to find out how her training has paid off; to find out if my wild little Madam is under control, if she can qualify in Working Trials, if she could get placed in Obedience.

Whether we compete or not, as long as she lives, I have to go on training her. I found, over Christmas, when we had to cope with a flooded home and the dogs simply had to be left with very little exercise, that Chita was wildly excited, restless and edgy. She hadn't had the opportunity to go out and use her brains, as I couldn't leave water on the floors and take the dogs for their training. It's years since a day went by without at least an hour's session with her. Usually it is longer. It is not all work, but it does stretch her active little brain. I've learned how to work out new routines for her, find new things for her to do – and she loves learning.

She spent a brief three days with our little grandson, who is only two years old. Jonathan fell off his chair and hit her accidentally, very hard, with his toy car. Had she been a wicked dog, she would have turned on him.

She looked at him in disbelief and came and leaned against me and put her paw on me.

"Did you see what he did? Did he mean it?"

I re-assured her, and she went to her bed. She watched him play and took care to keep her distance next time he sat up for a meal, in case he fell and hit her again. He hadn't meant to fall; he was as dismayed as she was.

I must remember I am Pack Leader. A word, a signal, at home or out, and they obey. That is the way it has to be for the rest of Chita's life. Not to show off my personality, but to make sure my imp never again gets the upper hand. And if I relax or she is with someone less dominant than she, she plays up. Behave, little bitch!

Time for lunch. Time to stop typing, time to open the door. Time to relax; and as I put away my typewriter, I know that as always my first words as I stand up will be "Behave, little bitch!"

THE END